RIDING COLORADO

Day Trips From Denver With Your Horse

by
Margi Evans

Photography by
Lynn Johnson

With special thanks to our "Test Riders"
and husbands.

Contact the author at our website:
www.ridingcoloradotrails.com

First Printing-2005
Second Printing-2005
Revised and Third Printing-2006

Printed in the U.S A. by
King Printing Co., Inc.
181 Industrial Ave.
Lowell, MA 01852-5147

CONTENTS

Introduction

While I was born in Oregon and lived my first 44 years there, I am actually a misplaced Coloradoan! I realized this as soon as I moved here and set about exploring my new home. I have visited nearly all the museums, zoos, gardens, government and historic sites in the Denver area. I loved them all. However, I discovered the best way to explore Colorado is on the back of my horse!

As often as possible, I line up some friends for a "Mom's Day Off." We make an extra lunch as we pack the school lunches and as the school bus pulls away, we load our horses in the trailer. Off we go to a trailhead to spend the day riding. We really can't imagine heaven being any better than this!

After exploring every trail we could find, I made a trip to the bookstore to find some new trails. I found books for hikes both near and far, books for hiking with your family, with your dog and on your mountain bike. But none for trail riding. So, I decided to research parks and open space areas and create one myself. However, my friends also wanted to be involved. So, I solicited their help as researchers and test riders. This book is the result of the most fun "homework" we've ever been assigned.

We designed this book to fit the needs of the horseman. So "Happy Trails to You!"

Using This Book

In order to get a consistent distance measurement of both miles and time, we decided we needed to start from the same spot for every ride. Since we all live in the Parker area, we decided to begin our distance measurements from the intersection of I-25 and South Lincoln. So if you are reading this in Boulder, please take that into account.

We took all levels of riders on these trails to test ride them. However, it is up to each rider to use caution and wisdom on all trail rides. No horse is totally "bomb proof" but all horses should be well trained and under the rider's control at all times.

Acknowledgements

Throughout a year and a half of research for this book, I have placed many calls to the county parks departments. Without exception, I have found them to be extremely informative and eager to help me have a successful experience in the parks and open spaces of which they are so proud. A special note of gratitude goes to Janet Bellis in Boulder County, Jackie Sanderson in Douglas County, Brian Kay in El Paso County, Bridgit Silver in Jefferson County and Scott Dollus with the U.S. Forest Service for help with the maps. State Parks trail maps were secured off the Internet with permission.

Information on the history of the parks has been found on materials supplied on the Internet by the state and county parks departments.

Additional thanks go to Atieh Helton and Steven Jones for their technical expertise. Tieh spent many late nights helping me navigate the computer! Additional thanks go to Melissa Rivera and Berniece Johnson for their editing help.

LIFE IS MUCH TOO SHORT
NOT TO RIDE IN COLORADO!

MEET THE TEST RIDERS

MARGI EVANS-author
Margi began taking English riding lessons as an 8 year old in Portland, Oregon. She saved her money and purchased her first horse at 13 and spent years competing in Pony Club and Hunter/ Jumper Shows. Margi graduated from Oregon State University and married her high school sweetheart in

1972. The newlywed budget forced the sale of her wonderful horse. After a twenty-five year break from equestrian sports to rear her five children and a move to Colorado, she purchased her thoroughbred, Kit, and a large pony, Hardee. She started focusing her energy on studying and competing in Dressage. Margi could not have completed this book without the help of her husband, Tom, and her "Test Riders!"

LYNN JOHNSON-photographer

Lynn, a native Texan, moved to Colorado in December of 2002. Lynn has ridden off and on throughout her life but has found a renewed appreciation for riding now that she has the beautiful foothills and mountains of Colorado in which to ride. When she isn't in the saddle or running with her dogs, she and her husband, Philip are busy rearing four children. She just purchased her first horse, a 5 year old Morab, Knight.

CAROL CRISP

Carol is a long time Coloradoan and a great outdoor enthusiast. She has ridden horses all of her life. She started riding as a child in Montana. As a teenager in Colorado she worked as a guide for trail rides on the High Line Canal in exchange for the chance to ride the horses. She has competed in Gymcanas and rides nearly every discipline. She also has been certified as a therapeutic riding instructor through the North American Riding for the Handicapped Association and was the head riding instructor at Praying Hands Ranch Therapeutic Riding Center for six years.She especially enjoys competing in Endurance Rides. She and her husband, Larry, have three children.

NANCY MILEGER

Nancy has spent her entire life riding. She claims she never got off once she got in the saddle. As a child, her father

farmed with horses. She took a short break from horse ownership while she and her husband, Val, reared four children. She enjoys endurance rides. But her favorite thing is to ride her 25 year old Arabian, Kishta on our trail rides.

MARY LUCHERINI
Mary is a busy wife and mother of 5 children who enjoys the great outdoors from the back of a horse. Her riding experience has been limited to riding the hills on her family's southern Idaho farm. Mary, and her husband Lonnie, moved to Colorado from Ohio in 2003. She has loved riding the Rocky Mountain trails with us. In addition, she has been our social coordinator!

JODI ANDRIANAKOS
Riding horses had been a life-long dream of Jodi's which was fulfilled 8 years ago when she was able to move to horse property and buy her first horse. She has been a quick study and has bought and sold several horses while she searched for just the right one. She has finally decided that Tennessee Walkers are her horse of choice. She and her husband John are also busy with their three children.

In addition to the "official" test riders, several other friends, family members and even one husband joined us on some of our trail rides and the author thanks them for their input!

5

TRAIL LISTINGS BY DISTANCE

All distances were measured from the intersection of Lincoln Avenue and I-25 near Parker.

Trails within 1/2 hour drive:
Bluffs Regional Park
Bayou Gulch Park
Chatfield State Park
Cherry Creek State Park
Cherry Creek Trail at North Pinery Parkway
Columbine Open Space
Deer Creek Canyon Park
Glendale Farm Open Space
Greenland Open Space
Highline Canal Trailhead
Piney Creek Trail
Salisbury Equestrian Park
Sharptail Ridge Open Space
South Valley Park
Waterton Canyon

Trails within 1 hour driving time:
Alderfer/Three Sisters Open Space
Apex Park
Barr Lake State Park
Bear Creek Regional Park
Black Forest Regional Park
Crown Hill Park
Elk Meadow
Fox Run Regional Park
Garden of the Gods
Indian Creek
Lair O' the Bear
Matthews/Winters Park
Meyers Ranch Park
Mount Falcon Park

Mount Herman/Monument Preserve
New Santa Fe Trail
Palmer Park
Pine Valley Park
Reynolds Park Open Space
Rock Creek Farm
Van Bibber Park
White Ranch

Trails within 1 and 1/2 hour driving time:
Eldorado Canyon State Park
Fountain Creek Regional Park
Gold Camp Road
Golden Gate Canyon State Park
Hall Ranch
Heil Valley Ranch
Kenosha Pass
Manitou Section 16
Rabbit Mountain
St. Mary's Falls
Stratton Open Space
Walker Ranch

Trails within 2 hours driving time:
Dome Rock
Mueller State Park

Trails beyond 2 hours driving time:
North Fork Trail-Roosevelt National Forest

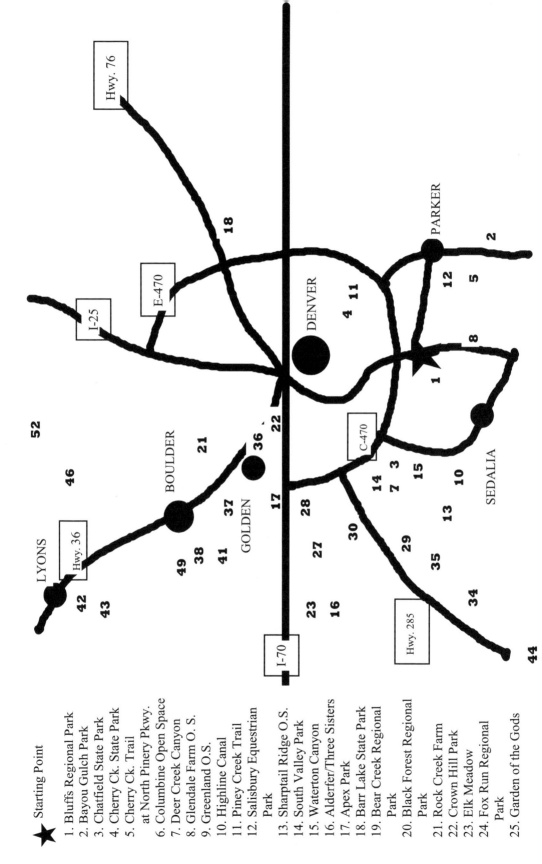

★ Starting Point

1. Bluffs Regional Park
2. Bayou Gulch Park
3. Chatfield State Park
4. Cherry Ck. State Park
5. Cherry Ck. Trail
   at North Pinery Pkwy.
6. Columbine Open Space
7. Deer Creek Canyon
8. Glendale Farm O. S.
9. Greenland O.S.
10. Highline Canal
11. Piney Creek Trail
12. Salisbury Equestrian
    Park
13. Sharptail Ridge O.S.
14. South Valley Park
15. Waterton Canyon
16. Alderfer/Three Sisters
17. Apex Park
18. Barr Lake State Park
19. Bear Creek Regional
    Park
20. Black Forest Regional
    Park
21. Rock Creek Farm
22. Crown Hill Park
23. Elk Meadow
24. Fox Run Regional
    Park
25. Garden of the Gods

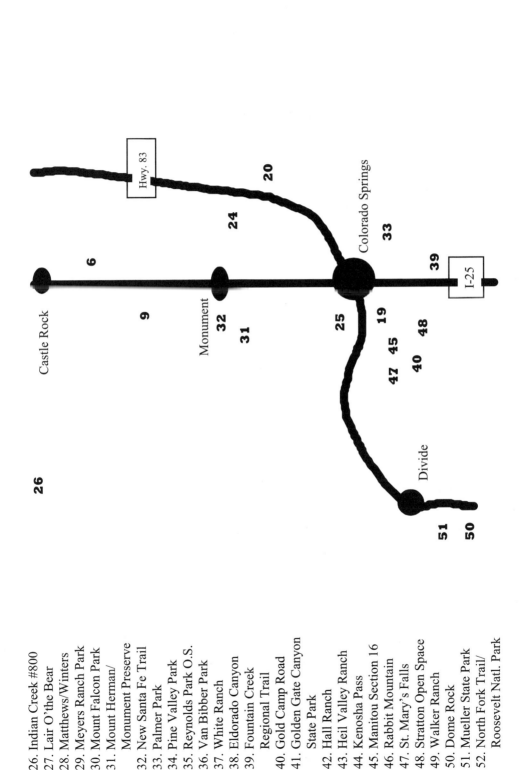

FAVORITES:

THE "BE SURE NOT TO MISS" TRAILS OR "FOUR HORSESHOES UP!"

Alderfer/Three Sisters Open Space-Jefferson County
Dome Rock-Teller County- (Open from July 16th to November 30th)
Hall Ranch-Boulder County
Fox Run Regional Park-El Paso County
Gold Camp Road- El Paso County
Garden of the Gods-El Paso County
Kenosha Pass-Park County
Matthews/Winters Park-Red Rocks Trail-Jefferson County
Mt. Falcon-Jefferson County
North Fork Trail-Roosevelt National Forest-Larimer County
Palmer Park-El Paso County
South Valley Park-Jefferson County
White Ranch-Jefferson County

FAVORITE FALL RIDES:
Deer Creek Canyon Park-Jefferson County
Elk Meadow Park-Jefferson County
Kenosha Pass-Park County
Indian Creek-Douglas County

WONDERFUL WINTER RIDES:
Barr Lake State Park-Adams County
Chatfield State Park-Douglas/Jefferson County
Cherry Creek Trail-Douglas County
Fountain Creek Regional Park-El Paso County
Greenland Open Space-Douglas County
Highline Canal-Douglas County
Rabbit Mountain-Boulder County
Rock Creek Farm-Boulder County
Sharptail Ridge Open Space-Douglas County

10

RIDING COLORADO

ADAMS COUNTY

Map from the State Parks website.

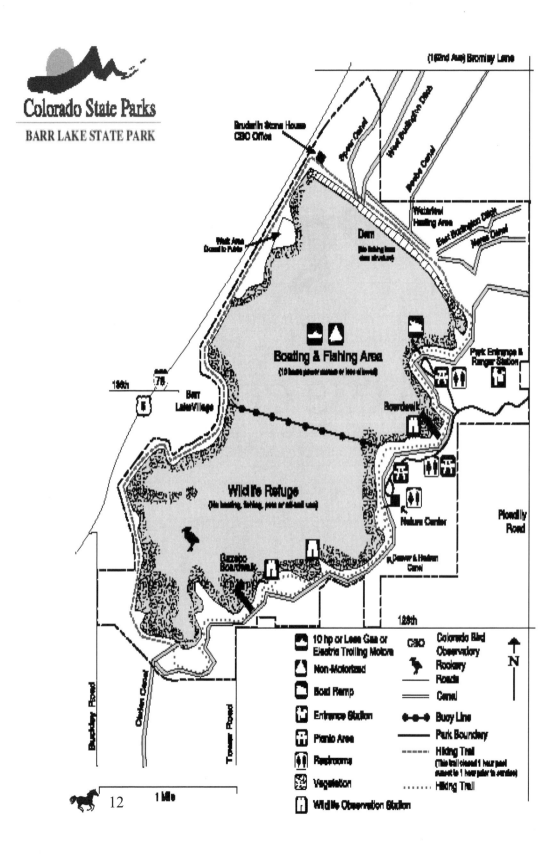

Barr Lake State Park - Adams County

Travel Distance: 40.5 miles

Travel Time: 1 hour

Travel Directions: Go east on Lincoln for 5.5 miles. Turn left onto Parker Road. Follow Parker Road for 10.4 miles. Take the I-225 North exit. Drive 8 miles north on I-225 to I-70. Go east on I-70 for 0.8 miles to Pena Blvd. Go north on Pena Blvd. for 2.5 miles to the 56th Street exit. Go east on 56th Street for 0.8 miles to Tower Road. Go north on Tower Road for 9.1 miles. Go east on 128th for 2 miles. Go north on Piccadilly Road for 1.1 miles. The park entrance is on your left. Barr Lake State Park may also be reached by driving north on I-76 toward Brighton. Take the Bromley Lane exit. Go east 1 mile to Picadilly. Go south on Picadilly for 1.9 miles. The entrance is on your right.

Trailer Parking: After entering the park and paying your fees, proceed to the boat ramp area. It has a large paved lot with painted spaces for 25 trailers. Now, I know these are intended to be shared with the boaters, but there is plenty of room for all of us. This area also has lots of picnic tables and grills.

Fees: $5.00

Water: Yes.

Restroom: Yes, very nice and year-round.

Length of Ride: 8.8 miles to circle the lake.

Hazards: The trail runs right next to a train track along a part of the northwest section of the lake for about a mile. A barbed wire fence is on the east side of 1/3 of this section of trail, the lake and a steep bank is on the east side of another 1/3 of this section. Only about 1/3 of this section of trail that runs along the track has a small amount of space on the east side of the trail to get away from the track. The first time we rode this section was in the morning, and we didn't see any sign of a train. However the second time we came to the park, we cleared this area and started back east away from the track at 1:15 p.m. At 1:18 p.m., a long train went by at high speed. Within 15 minutes a second train went by, and shortly there-after, a third train went by. The park ranger said that there is no regular schedule for the trains. For this reason, I recommend you NOT ride this part of the trail. A better plan would be to ride north, pass the dam and turn back around at the train track. Or go south in a clockwise direction until you come to the train track and turn around. Or do both, but stay away from the train track! There are also some bridges to cross. The west side of the lake is usually quite deserted. Most of the hikers, bird watchers and picnickers are on the east side of the lake. You will come across a lot of wildlife such as coyotes, deer and birds of prey, including bald eagles in the winter.

Description of our ride: We began our ride by going counter-clockwise on the trail that goes around the lake. Horses must take the trail below the dam. We found the trail is very easy going. It is mostly soft dirt with some patches of gravel. It is wide enough for two abreast which makes it a great place to train a pack horse. When we arrived at the train track, we checked both ways then trotted the nearly 1 mile that went beside the track. We used the bridges to cross the canals. The park ranger requests that riders use the bridges rather than make water crossings and that you not attempt to water horses in the lake or canals as the edges are very soft and much of the lake is a wildlife refuge. It took us 2.5 hours at a walk and trot the first time we rode around the lake and less than 2 hours at a trot and canter pace the second time we rode the trail.

This 2500-acre park is open year-round and is a great place to go on a pleasant winter day. Insects are heavy in the summer due to all of the water. Keep your eye out for the nesting eagles in the winter and for the other 330 species of birds!

Nancy, Margi, Jodi and Carol celebrate Jodi's birthday at Barr Lake!

RIDING COLORADO

ARAPAHOE COUNTY

Map from the State Parks website.

CHERRY CREEK STATE PARK

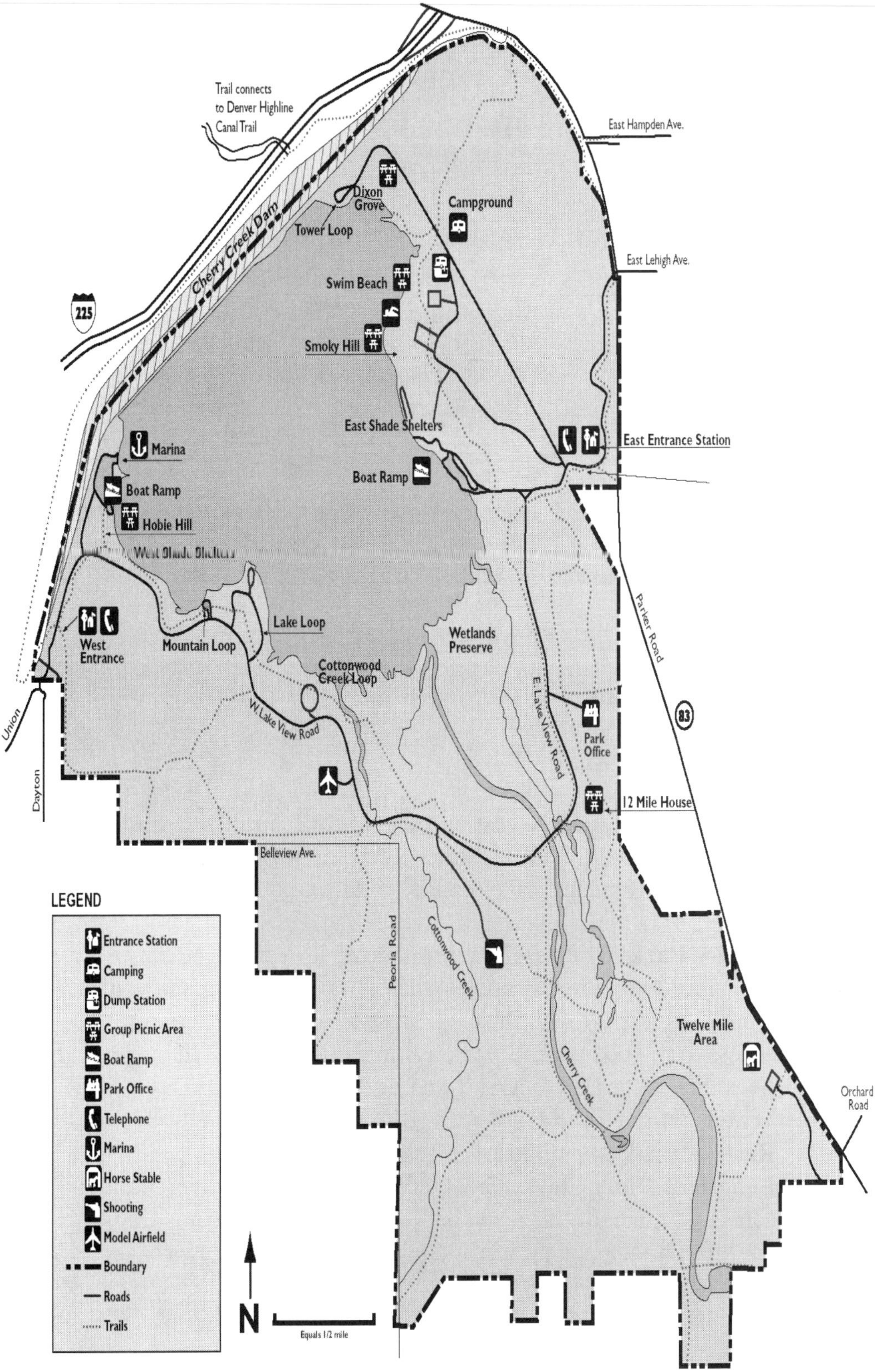

Trail connects to Denver Highline Canal Trail

East Hampden Ave.

Cherry Creek Dam

Dixon Grove

Tower Loop

Campground

East Lehigh Ave.

Swim Beach

Smoky Hill

East Shade Shelters

East Entrance Station

Marina

Boat Ramp

Boat Ramp

Hobie Hill

West Shade Shelters

Parker Road

Lake Loop

West Entrance

Mountain Loop

Wetlands Preserve

Cottonwood Creek Loop

W Lake View Road

E. Lake View Road

Park Office

83

12 Mile House

Union

Dayton

Belleview Ave.

Peoria Road

Cottonwood Creek

Cherry Creek

Twelve Mile Area

Orchard Road

LEGEND

- Entrance Station
- Camping
- Dump Station
- Group Picnic Area
- Boat Ramp
- Park Office
- Telephone
- Marina
- Horse Stable
- Shooting
- Model Airfield
- ▬ ▬ Boundary
- ── Roads
- ···· Trails

N

Equals 1/2 mile

Cherry Creek State Park - Arapahoe County

Travel Distance: 11 miles
Travel Time: 20 minutes
Travel Directions: Go east on Lincoln for 5.5 miles. Turn left onto Parker Road. Follow Parker Road for 5.4 miles. Turn left on Orchard Road and take the first right into the park.

Trailer Parking: There is a dirt parking lot where you may park. However, there is no designated trailer parking and you must share the lot with the cars, most of which are there for access to the dog park. Some days it is completely full!
Fees: $6 Labor Day to May 1 and $7 May 1 to Labor Day.
Water: No
Restroom: Yes outhouse
Length of Ride: Cherry Creek State Park contains over 3,500 acres and much of this is available for trail riding. Some trails go through the open prairie and provide beautiful views of the

 18

city and the mountains while others go along the creek through large cottonwoods. Spend the day or just a couple of hours.

Hazards: The trailer parking area and some of the riding area is shared with the dog park. The dog park has become very popular, especially on the weekends and after 5:00 p.m. A rifle range is used every day in the southwest section of the park. There is a model airfield in the southwest area of the park. There are a few water crossings and road crossings. A large herd of deer might jump out and surprise you. Trails are used by hikers and bikers also.

Description of our ride: We began our ride by going north through the dog park and past the Paint Horse Stable's pastures. We rode up to the Twelve Mile House picnic area then up to the park office to pick up some materials. From the office we learned that we could ride anywhere except in the wetlands preserve directly to our west or on the lake beaches. We then followed the trail back south around the preserve, back to the dog park and rode west. We took a lovely trail along the creek bed and through large cottonwoods. We saw deer and birds. At one point, the trail went close to the rifle range. The rifle sounds made some of our horses quite nervous. The trail crossed West Lake View road and headed toward the west side of the park. There the trail went close to a model airfield that is used heavily on the weekends. Coming back, we came across some dogs that were not under their owner's control. This may be a big concern for many of you if your horse is not accustomed to aggressive behavior from dogs. You must realize that these urban parks and trails will have a lot of hazards that can frighten your horse so either make sure you are on your toes and don't ride alone or take a horse that is "bomb proof," which mine are not! Trails are either packed sand or dirt. Shoes are not required and, since the park is quite flat, any horse could handle it.

See Piney Creek Trail for another day's experience at Cherry Creek State Park.

Cherry Creek State Park was established in 1959 around the dam and reservoir that were built in 1950 by the U.S. Army Corps to control flooding. This area was part of the Smoky Hill Trail that was used by thousands of pioneers from 1859 to 1865 as they traveled to the mountains to search for gold. This area was also heavily logged in the latter half of the 19th century and once supported the first purebred cattle industry within the state. It is now one of the state's most popular parks with approximately 1.5 million visitors a year. Group campsites may be reserved for camping with your horse.

Piney Creek Trail - Arapahoe County

Travel Distance: 11 miles
Travel Time: 20 minutes
Travel Directions: Go east on Lincoln for 5.5 miles. Turn left onto Parker Road. Follow Parker Road for 5.4 miles. Turn right on Orchard Road and take the first right into the shopping center parking lot.

Trailer Parking: This is a paved parking lot that the park shares with the shopping center. There is no designated trailer parking and you must share the lot with the cars. Parking could become a major problem if those stores fill up.
Fees: none
Water: No
Restroom: No, you would have to ride over to Cherry Creek State Park to find a restroom or outhouse.
Length of Ride: Going east you can ride for over 4 miles until you reach Liverpool Road. Going west you can get into Cherry Creek State Park and can ride for miles.

Hazards: City hazards like traffic along Orchard Road, construction and heavy equipment being used by whomever is building the new recreation center, joggers and dogs on leashes, bridges. In the park see the hazards listed on the Cherry Creek State Park evaluation.

Description of our ride: We started our ride to the east but soon decided that the traffic along Orchard Road and construction machinery were too much for us. We were riding beside a paved bike path. If Arapahoe county really wants to cater to equestrians, it needs to make a separate trail closer to the creek and away from the traffic. Perhaps this will happen in the future. At this time, I would not recommend this trail unless your horse is used to lots of traffic.

After returning to the parking lot, we decided to investigate the west route into Cherry Creek State Park. We had to cross under Parker Road. The underpass is low for a horse as big as mine and scary with all the traffic. If you can get past that, you are in for a lovely ride. The trail to the park borders a neighborhood and crosses over the creek on wooden bridges. In places you have to ride along the paved bike path. In other areas you can ride beside it. The trail leads to the southernmost part of Cherry Creek State Park. This area is below the dog park and, except for a few bikers, we had the fields and trails to ourselves. We crossed a bridge and took a loop to the left, although the trail was hard to find in a few places. We then rode north on a trail that runs parallel to Jordan Road. This part of the road is closed now so we saw no traffic. We crossed the road and went through a gate into the field on the west side of Jordan Road. Some of the Paint Horse Stable's horses were grazing there. Watch out for a fallen barbed wire fence. This is a huge field and a wonderful place to ride.

Our experience in this part of Cherry Creek State Park was completely different than our previous visit! See Cherry Creek State Park.

 22

BOULDER COUNTY

Maps courtesy of Boulder County Department of Parks
and Open Space

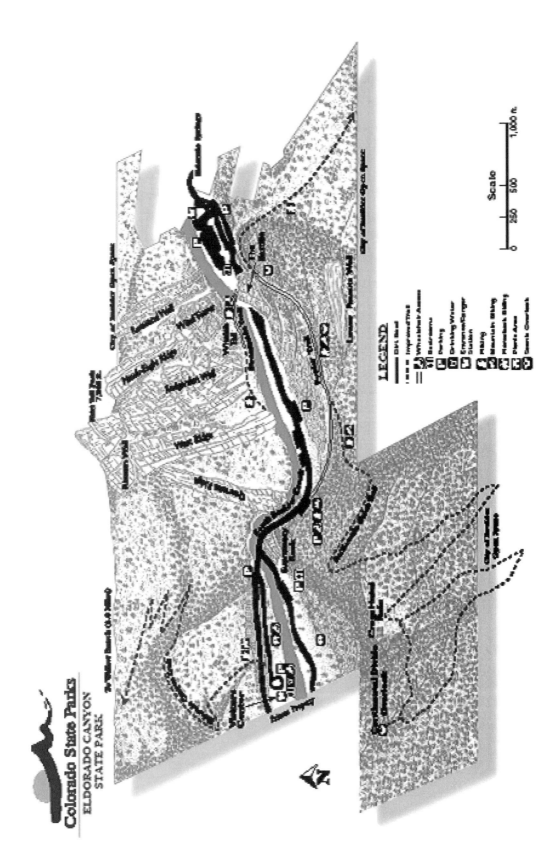

Eldorado Canyon State Park - Boulder County

Travel Distance: 45.4 miles
Travel Time: 1 hour and 14 minutes
Travel Directions: From Lincoln, go north on I-25 for 23.8 miles to the Hwy. 36 exit to Boulder. Go west on Hwy. 36 for 14.1 miles to the "Louisville-Superior" exit. At the top of the exit, turn left. After crossing the highway, turn right at the light onto Hwy 170. You will follow Hwy 170 for 7.3 miles following the signs to Eldorado Springs. When you come to the little town of Eldorado Springs, the pavement ends and becomes a pothole filled dirt road. The road ends at the park entrance.

Trailer Parking: Do not try coming on a weekend as you will not be able to find a parking spot for a trailer! The best trailer option is to turn right into the lower lot just after the park ranger booth at the entrance. This has the biggest area in which to turn around. If no one is there, there is room for 3 or

4 trailers.

Fees: $6.00

Water: Yes, up by the visitor's center. There is also access to South Boulder Creek for your horses.

Restrooms: Yes, outhouse by the parking lot, very nice bathrooms at the visitor's center.

Length of Ride: We rode for 3 hours and covered 4 miles.

Hazards: This is an extremely rugged trail with lots of rocky steps and rock faces to cross. This is a popular trail for mountain bikes. You will also come across hikers, dogs on leashes, rock climbers and bridges.

Description of our ride: Make sure your horses are shod and in good condition before tackling this one! The views are spectacular but the trail is not easy going! The only trail that is open to horses is the Eldorado Canyon Trail. It climbs 1,000 rugged feet and ends after 4.5 miles at the Pika road within Boulder County Park's Walker Ranch. We began from the lower parking lot and rode along the road that runs between the cliffs and the river. Our horses saw their first rock climbers that looked like giant spiders sliding down their webs! After nearly a half mile, we crossed a river. Here the road splits. To the left is the visitor's center and a lovely picnic area. The road to the right leads to the trailhead. The first mile of the trail is a steep climb. In some places we went up man made steps and in other places we had to negotiate rocks. We had to go slowly! But it is fun riding slowly as the views are fabulous. We watched four trains weave around the ridges to our north on the Denver and Rio Grande Railroad. After a steady climb, the trail levels off a bit but remains rocky for a while. If you can get over the rocks, you come to a section of trail that was nice packed dirt. We stopped here for lunch. We then turned around and made our way slowly down. The trail continues and drops sharply down to the river. Just before crossing the river you can turn right and take the Walker Ranch loop, which is another 7.5 miles for the complete loop. However, the Boulder Parks Department does not recommend riding this loop as there are 500 feet of steps at one point. If you go to the left you cross part of the Walker Ranch area and re-enter the Crescent Meadows area of Eldorado State Park.

This photo shows you how treacherous this trail can be!

Hall Ranch

NORTH FOOTHILLS OPEN SPACE

Hall Family Brand

LOCATION MAP

Area Enlarged

Hall Ranch

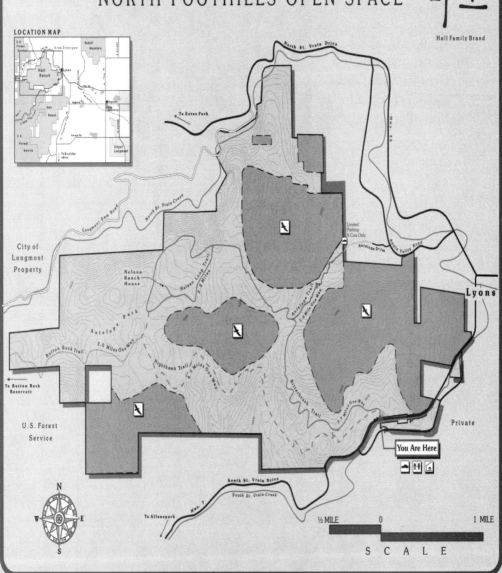

City of
Longmont
Property

Nelson
Ranch
House

To Estes Park

North St. Vrain Drive

Hwy. 36

Limited
Parking
8 Cars Only

Antelope Drive

Apple Valley Road

Lyons

Nelson Loop Trail
2.2 Miles

Antelope Trail
1.3 Mile One Way

Antelope Park

2.0 Miles One Way

Button Rock Trail

To Button Rock
Reservoir

Nighthawk Trail
1.4 Miles One Way

Bitterbrush Trail
3.7 Mile One Way

You Are Here

U.S. Forest
Service

Private

North St. Vrain Creek

Longmont Dam Road

South St. Vrain Drive

South St. Vrain Creek

To Allenspark

Hwy. 7

N
W — E
S

½ MILE   0   1 MILE

SCALE

 PARKING

 RESTROOMS

PICNIC SHELTER

 MULTI-USE TRAIL
(PEDESTRIANS, EQUESTRIANS, BIKES)

 NO BICYCLES

PEDESTRIAN TRAIL

 INTERMITTENT STREAM

UNPAVED ROAD

PAVED ROAD

 CRITICAL WILDLIFE HABITAT
NO PUBLIC ACCESS

 Boulder
County

1/2004

Hall Ranch - Boulder County

Travel Distance: 67.4 miles
Travel Time: 1 hour and 30 minutes
Travel Directions: From Lincoln, go north on I-25 for 50 miles to the Hwy 66 exit, Lyons exit #243. At the top of the exit, turn left (west) onto Highway 66. Once you are in Lyons, this becomes a one-way onto 36. After 16 miles you will be at a light in Lyons at which you must turn left or right. Go left onto Highway 7 for 1.4 miles. The trailhead is on your right. Go up to the upper parking lot where there are 5 trailer parking spaces.

Trailer Parking: There are five very nice drive-through parking spots for trailers with hitching posts between them. The lot is gravel and has an easy turn around.
Fees: No
Water: Not at the trailhead, but there is a spring-fed trough at the Nelson Homestead for horses.

Restrooms: Yes, outhouse
Length of Ride: We rode for 4 hours and covered 10.6 miles.
Hazards: Some round rocks on parts of the trail. Hikers, bikers, no dogs allowed at this time, one bridge, lots of wildlife.

Description of our ride: This was one of our favorite trails! Hall Ranch is a spectacularly beautiful park comprising 3,205 acres of Boulder County's foothills. It ranges from 5,440 feet to 6,820 feet in elevation. We started our ride by taking the Nighthawk Trail. We rode over hills and through beautiful meadows and enjoyed views of Longs Peak and Mt. Meeker. This was a narrow, packed, dirt, easy trail even though it continually climbed upward. After about 4 miles of walking, trotting and cantering, we came across a place in the trail where an old road curves to the right and the dirt trail goes to the left past a water trough and into the woods. You are supposed to go to the left though it is not marked clearly. After going through the woods and back into a meadow and back into woods, we came out in a high meadow. The Bottom Rock Trail goes off to the left. This is a foot trail only. We continued on until we reached the Nelson Loop Trail. We took it to the right and stopped at the old Nelson Ranch House for lunch. What a fabulous stop for lunch. Our horses enjoyed the meadow grass and the fresh water trough and we enjoyed the views. We were visiting this park in the fall and were treated to an elk bugle. We saw several deer and a coyote. After lunch, we rode back by way of the Nelson Loop Trail to the Bitterbrush Trail. This trail is much rockier and more challenging than the easy Nighthawk Trail. However, the rocks are not sharp or loose so they were not bad. I would say it is only medium in difficulty. If you are concerned, go up the Bitterbrush Trail and down the Nighthawk trail. On our way down we passed the Prairie Dog town that Boulder has established and saw more deer. This is a wonderful place to ride...don't miss it!

Hall Ranch was one of the first purchases made by Boulder

County after voters approved an open space sales tax in 1993. What a blessing for all of us! Before that, more than 20 families are known to have lived and worked on this land. There is an interesting history written up on a sign by the Nelson Farm House. All that now remains of the Nelson's ranch is the crumbling house, a cement block silo, and a still-functioning spring-fed water trough.

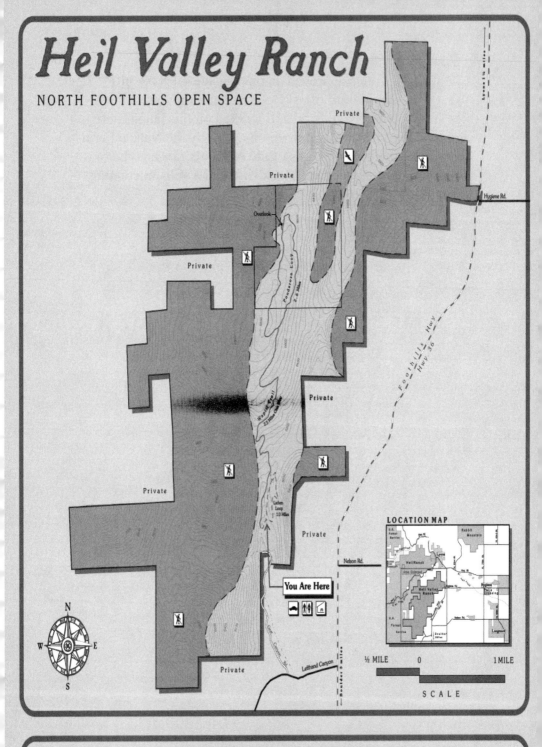

Heil Valley Ranch

NORTH FOOTHILLS OPEN SPACE

Private

Private

Private

Private

Private

Private

Private

Private

Private

Overlook

Ponderosa Loop
2.6 Miles

Wapiti Trail
2.5 Miles One Way

Lichen
Loop
1.0 Miles

Hygiene Rd.

Foothills Hwy
Hwy 36

Lyons 11 Miles

Nelson Rd.

Lefthand Canyon

You Are Here

LOCATION MAP

Rabbit Mountain

Heil Ranch

Heil Valley Ranch

Lyons

Hygiene

Boulder

Longmont

½ MILE   0   1 MILE

S C A L E

N
W E
S

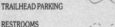

Heil Valley Ranch - Boulder County

Travel Distance: 67.4 miles
Travel Time: 1 hour and 15 minutes
Travel Directions: From Lincoln, go north on I-25 for miles 23.8 to the Highway 36 exit. Go west on 36 for 29.7 miles. Go through Boulder and continue north. Look for a sign that says "Ward and Jamestown" right before the Greenbriar Restaurant, which is a little, green building hidden behind trees on your left. Turn left onto Lefthand Drive. Go west for 0.65 miles to Geer Canyon Road. Turn right onto this dirt road and go for 1.1 miles. The trailhead is on your right.

Trailer Parking: This is the prettiest trailhead we have seen! It is nestled in between tall pines with a stream running alongside. It is a large gravel lot with lots of room for 4 or 5 trailers at the top side. Hitching posts are provided.
Fees: No
Water: There is a stream that runs between the parking lot and the picnic area for water for your horses.
Restrooms: Yes, outhouse

Length of Ride: We rode for 2.5 hours and covered 7.5 miles.

Hazards: The trail is very rocky with very little space to trot or canter. Hikers, bikers, but no dogs allowed at this time, one bridge, lots of wildlife.

Description of our ride: This is Boulder County's newest park. It was purchased with lottery funds. It covers 4,932 acres and has 7.8 miles of trails, most of which are available to ride. The ranch has an interesting history. From 1913 to 1917, this ranch was used to reintroduce elk to Boulder County. A very beautiful but rocky trail takes you up a gentle climb through the forest. We took the right side of the loop, which takes you over the ridge and gives you beautiful views of the Continental Divide. You are also looking over at Hall Ranch Open Space. We finished the loop after having lunch at the top and rode back down the trail and back to the parking lot. You can't get lost as there is only one route to follow! This is great for a slow, relaxing ride.

Shoes are recommended.

Rabbit Mountain - Boulder County

Travel Distance: 66.4 miles
Travel Time: 1 hour and 30 minutes
Travel Directions: From Lincoln, go north on I-25 for 50 miles to the Hwy. 66 exit, Lyons exit #243. At the top of the exit, turn left (west) onto Hwy. 66. Travel west on Hwy. 66 for 13.4 miles to 53rd Street. This is a small road so watch for it. Go north for 3 miles. The trailhead is on your right.

Trailer Parking: There are 4 back-in trailer parking spots with nice hitching posts. The lot is gravel and an easy turn around.
Fees: No
Water: No
Restrooms: Yes, outhouse
Length of Ride: We rode for 2 hours and covered 5.5 miles.
Hazards: This is a very rocky trail. Shoes are a must. Hikers, bikers, dogs on leashes, wildlife.

Description of our ride: Rabbit Mountain is of unique

geological interest as it sits three miles east of the rest of the foothills. As such, it is easily visible from three counties and gives the rider beautiful views of the plains to the east and the mountains to the west. From the parking lot, we rode northeast then turned directly north and rode up the Little Thompson Overlook Trail to its end. Out and back on this trail is 1.6 miles. We then rode back and took the Eagle Wind Trail in a counterclockwise direction. This trail takes you through some pretty wooded areas. It isn't quite as rocky as the Overlook Trail. As you ride, look for both mule deer and white-tailed deer. This is one of the few areas in Colorado where both types of deer can be found. There was also a bald eagle circling around the day we were there. Rattlesnakes are common at Rabbit Mountain, but they will do everything possible to avoid you. This trail is one of the hottest in the summer because it has little shade and lots of rock. For this reason it is considered a good winter trail as the snow melts quickly here. Spring, fall and winter are the best times to ride here. Be sure to have shoes on your horse. Other than the rocks, it is an easy trail, and the views in all directions are beautiful.

Rabbit Mountain was sold to Boulder County in 1984 by the granddaughter of the mountain's second owner, Jack Moormaw. Mr. Moormaw was a forest ranger with a strong desire to preserve the wilderness. I'm sure he would be happy that the mountain is now a lovely 1,479-acre park. Boulder takes beautiful care of this park.

Rock Creek Farm
Boulder County

Travel Distance: 38.6 miles
Travel Time: 55 minutes
Travel Directions: From Lincoln Avenue, drive north on I-25 for 24 miles to the Hwy. 36 exit toward Boulder. Drive west on Hwy. 36 for 9 miles to the Broomfield/Hwy. 287 exit. Drive north on Hwy. 287 for 2.9 miles. Turn left onto Dillon Road. Stay to the right to avoid getting on the parkway. Drive west on Dillon Road for 1 mile. Turn left onto 104. The parking lot is 0.7 miles ahead on the left.

Trailer parking: There is a nice dirt parking lot with room for 1 or 2 trailers.
Fees: None
Water: No
Restrooms: Yes, porta-potty
Length of Ride: Our ride was interrupted by a rain and wind storm so we only covered 3.8 miles in 1 hour.

Hazards: Hikers, dogs on leashes, 1 bridge, 1 gate on the road. This is a working farm so there will be farm equipment being used.

Description of Our Ride: From the parking lot, we rode toward the lake and followed the Mary Miller Trail around the lake until it turns north. It ran between the cultivated fields until it came to a temporary dead-end. (Be sure to ride the loop at the end!) Plans are in the works to extend the trail north from this point. At the time of our ride, the Mary Miller trail is 1.6 miles long to the current end. We then turned around and followed the trail back to the south side of the lake and the junction with the Cradleboard Trail. This trail is 1.3 miles to the end. We started out on the trail but, due to a storm, we took the short cut to the right, through the gate and back up the road to the parking lot.

This is a wonderful place to ride any time of year. It is so quiet! Just take a minute and listen to the quiet. The trail is either packed dirt or gravel so shoes would not be necessary. It is a very easy trail and great for beginning riders and horses.

Note: The first two printings of *Riding Colorado* included the wonderful Coal Creek Trail on the recommendation of the Boulder County Open Space staff. However, after the book was published, the city of Louisville took over the maintenance of the parking lot and will not allow horses on the part of the trail that goes across their property. Those of you in Boulder County should try to get that changed. So, I decided to replace that trail with the Rock Creek Farm trail. I know you will very much enjoy riding on this working farm.

Walker Ranch

SOUTH BOULDER CREEK TRAILHEAD

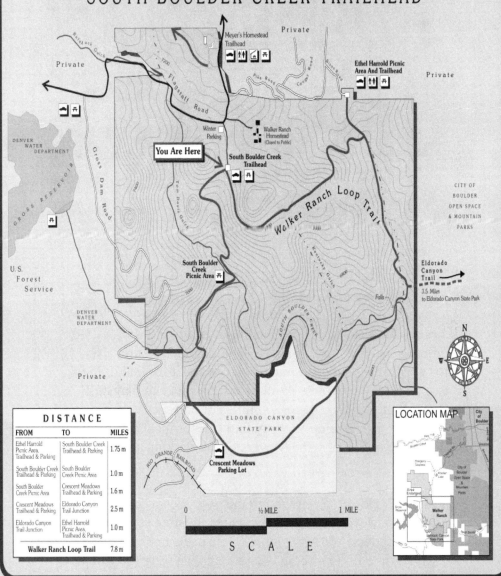

Meyer's Homestead Trailhead

Private

Ethel Harrold Picnic Area And Trailhead

Private

Private

Winter Parking

Walker Ranch Homestead (Closed to Public)

You Are Here

South Boulder Creek Trailhead

Walker Ranch Loop Trail

CITY OF BOULDER OPEN SPACE & MOUNTAIN PARKS

DENVER WATER DEPARTMENT

GROSS RESERVOIR

South Boulder Creek Picnic Area

Eldorado Canyon Trail

3.5 Miles to Eldorado Canyon State Park

U.S. Forest Service

DENVER WATER DEPARTMENT

Falls

SOUTH BOULDER CREEK

Private

N W E S

ELDORADO CANYON STATE PARK

LOCATION MAP

RIO GRANDE RAILROAD

Crescent Meadows Parking Lot

DISTANCE

FROM	TO	MILES
Ethel Harrold Picnic Area. Trailhead & Parking	South Boulder Creek Trailhead & Parking	1.75 m
South Boulder Creek Trailhead & Parking	South Boulder Creek Picnic Area	1.0 m
South Boulder Creek Picnic Area	Crescent Meadows Trailhead & Parking	1.6 m
Crescent Meadows Trailhead & Parking	Eldorado Canyon Trail Junction	2.5 m
Eldorado Canyon Trail Junction	Ethel Harrold Picnic Area. Trailhead & Parking	1.0 m
Walker Ranch Loop Trail		**7.8 m**

0   ½ MILE   1 MILE

S C A L E

PARKING	⋯⋯ INTERMITTENT STREAM
RESTROOMS	—— PAVED ROAD
PICNIC SHELTER	—— UNPAVED ROAD
PICNIC TABLES	

〰 MULTIPLE USE TRAIL

ELDORADO CANYON TRAIL NO BICYCLES

Boulder County

Walker Ranch - Boulder County

Travel Distance: 45.4 miles
Travel Time: 1 hour and 30 minutes
Travel Directions: From Lincoln, go north on I-25 for 23.8 miles to the Highway 36 exit to Boulder. Go west on Hwy. 36 for 19.7 miles to the Baseline Road exit. At the end of the exit go left (West) onto Baseline for 2.0 miles to Flagstaff Road. Follow Flagstaff for 7.0 miles of narrow roads and hair-pin turns! The Boulder County Parks department recommends that horse trailers use the Meyers Gulch Parking area on your right.

Trailer Parking: Even though the parks department recommends the Meyers Gulch Parking area, it is not set up very well for trailers. We had a large goose neck and had a very difficult time finding room even though we were there on a weekday and there were few cars. The problem is that they have divided the parking spaces with timbers so we couldn't just park across several car spots. If you had a smaller trailer, there were a few spots that seemed long enough to back into in such a way that you would not be blocking the access. Each parking lot was circular so we just had to park parallel to the road on one of the turn-arounds. Boulder County needs to set up better trailer parking.

Fees: No

Water: No

Restrooms: Yes, outhouse

Length of Ride: We rode for 3 hours and covered 6 miles.

Hazards: Some round rocks on parts of the trail. Hikers, bikers, dogs on leashes.

Description of our ride: From the parking lot, we took the Meyers Homestead Trail. This was an easy trail. Much of it is an old fire road so it would be a good spot to pony a horse. About 0.5 miles up the trail, is a historic sawmill. The little path that leads to the mill is 0.3 miles and is a dead end. The main trail goes to the right. Farther up is to a lovely meadow in which stand the remains of a 1880's log cabin. The trail ends after 2.5 miles at a beautiful rocky overlook with views of the peaks. This is where we stopped for lunch. On the way back we noticed a little-used road going off to the left. We followed it for over 0.5 miles to where it ended at Flagstaff Road. It is a pretty ride so I recommend this side trip. We went back down to the main trail, turned left and returned to the parking lot.

This is an easy trail with only a 600-foot climb in elevation. Shoes are always a good idea but not required here.

Walker Ranch has an interesting history. This area was settled in 1869 by James Walker who came to Colorado from Missouri for health reasons with just $12 in his pocket. As his health improved, so did his ranching skills. From the original claim of 160 acres, Mr. Walker expanded the ranch to 6,000 acres before selling it in 1959. This was one of the largest cattle ranches in this part of Colorado. Boulder County owns 2,566 acres of land. The ranch is listed on the National Register of Historic Places.

41

RIDING COLORADO

DOUGLAS COUNTY

Maps courtesy of Douglas County Division of Open Space
and Natural Resources, State Parks Web Site
and The U.S Forest Service

Bayou Gulch Park - Douglas County

Travel Distance: 12.9 miles
Travel Time: 20 minutes
Travel Directions: Go east on Lincoln Avenue for 5.5 miles
to Parker Road. Go south on Parker Road for 7.1 miles to
Bayou Gulch (there is a light and Ponderosa High School is
on your left.) Stay in the right of the two turn lanes. Go east
on Bayou Gulch Road for 1.5 miles. Turn left on Fox Sparrow
and drive north for 0.2 miles. The horse trailer parking is on
your right.

Trailer Parking: The gravel parking lot has spaces for 5 or 6
trailers.
Fees: None
Water: No
Restrooms: Yes, outhouse
Length of Ride: 3 miles if you ride both the outer loop and
the inner one.

Hazards: Walkers, bikers, dogs on leases, one road crossing on the outer loop.

Description of our ride: This is a fairly new park with a lovely, wide, packed sand trail. You will get beautiful views of the front range from Pikes Peak to Longs Peak. We took the trail in a clockwise direction. It goes down a gentle slope toward Bayou Gulch Road. You have to cross Fox Sparrow Road so don't be there when the middle school is letting out! Most of the time, there is no traffic on this little road. We crossed the road and rode toward the Colorado Horse Park, climbed the hill, and stopped to enjoy the beautiful view of the mountains. The trail then goes north to the back side of the school and back to the parking lot. You can then start again and take the inner loop that does not cross the road. The two loops together are 3 miles. The trail is wide enough to ride two a breast or pony a horse. No shoes would be needed and it is a good place to condition your horse. We rode for about 45 minutes and covered both loops at a leisurely pace. Many riders who keep their horses at the Colorado Horse Park enjoy this park.

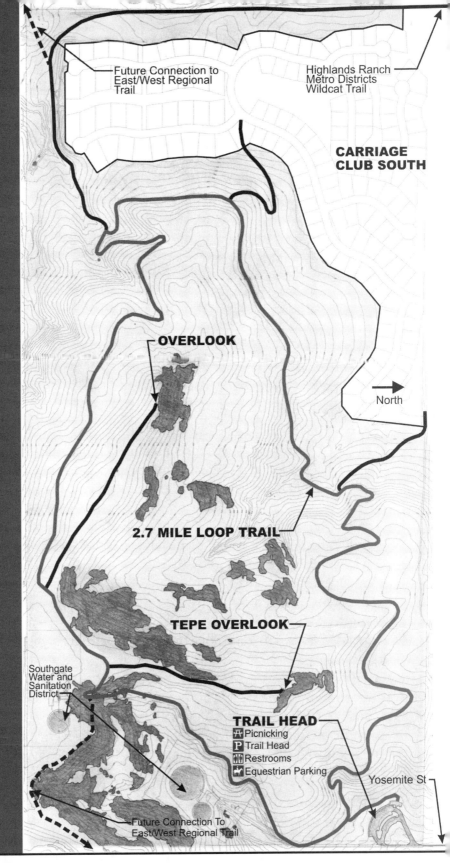

BLUFFS REGIONAL PARK

Future Connection to East/West Regional Trail

Highlands Ranch Metro Districts Wildcat Trail

CARRIAGE CLUB SOUTH

OVERLOOK

→ North

2.7 MILE LOOP TRAIL

TEPE OVERLOOK

Southgate Water and Sanitation District

TRAIL HEAD
A Picnicking
P Trail Head
Restrooms
Equestrian Parking

Yosemite St

Future Connection To East/West Regional Trail

Bluffs Regional Park - Douglas County

Travel Distance: 1.2 miles
Travel Time: 6 minutes
Travel Directions: Go west on Lincoln 0.8 miles to Ridgegate Parkway. Turn left and drive 0.1 mile. Turn right onto Crooked Stick Trail. Go 0.3 miles south to the park entrance.

Trailer Parking: The lower part of the parking lot is great for 4 or 5 trailers. Nice covered picnic area.
Fees: None
Water: No
Restrooms: Yes, Port-A-Potty
Length of Ride: 3.5 miles
Hazards: Hikers, bikers, dogs on leashes, warning signs about rattlesnakes.

Description of our ride: This is a new park with a lovely, wide, crushed granite trail. You will get beautiful views of the front range from Pikes Peak to Longs Peak. However, you have to look over a sea of roof tops that weren't there a few years

46

ago! This trail goes up a gentle slope to the top of the Bluffs. The loop is 2.7 miles. However, there are two side trails that go to overlooks. These give you the best views. The trail is wide enough to ride two abreast or pony a horse. No shoes would be needed and it is a good place to condition your horse. We rode for one hour and covered the loop and both overlook trails.

Colorado State Parks

CHATFIELD STATE PARK

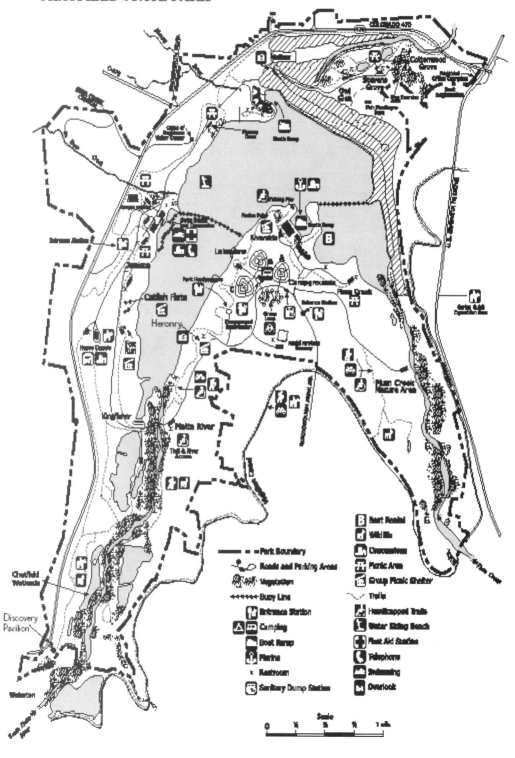

Chatfield State Park-
Douglas and Jefferson Counties

Travel Distance: 14.5 miles

Time: 15 minutes

Travel Directions: Go north on I-25 0.9 miles to the C-470 west exit. Drive for 12.1 miles west on C-470 to the Wadsworth exit. At the bottom of the exit, turn left onto Wadsworth. Travel one mile to the park entrance. The entrance is on your left.

Trailer Parking: A large paved parking lot for trailers with clearly marked spaces is provided. In addition to this, there are two public corrals for day or overnight use. Horses can be left there while the owners camp at the campground.

Fees: $5

Water: Yes

Restroom: Yes, outhouse and permanent restrooms

Length of Ride: There are over 24 miles of trails on which to ride. You can weave around the entire area at the south end of the reservoir on both sides of the South Platte River. Trails also connect with Waterton Canyon.

Hazards: Hikers and bikers. The dog park is easy to avoid by staying south. Search and rescue dogs are trained there as well. Water crossings across the South Platte River can be deep and swift. There is lots of wildlife.

Description of our ride: The day we went to test ride the trails at Chatfield was one of those days that make us all glad to be Coloradoans. It was 65 degrees under a bright blue sky with not a breath of wind...in January! After visiting with Sherry at Chatfield Stables, we rode around on the west side of the fenced pasture and picked up the trail going south toward the lake. There we stopped for a moment to watch the ice fishermen. We then took advantage of some other trail riders to lead us across the South Plate River crossing. It was quite swift and deep this time of year so some of the riders chose to go across the bridge. On the east side of the river, we found trails weaving all around, both across rolling hills and through beautiful forests. One trail along the river had a series of logs set up for jumping! We saw many other trail riders who either lived close by or kept their horses at the Cottonwood Stables. These riders had all ridden in. Several people were ponying a horse as the trails on the open hills are quite wide. The trails in the woods are only wide enough for one horse so ponying would difficult. Trails are either packed sand or dirt. Shoes are not required and, since the park's hills are not too steep, any horse could handle it. It was a beautiful winter Saturday when we were there so the park was quite busy. However, the riding trails seemed to be away from the rest of the crowds. After riding many of the trails on the east side of the river, we chose to go back up to the northern river crossing as the southern one had ice along the edge. We really felt that this park was a fabulous place to ride. We thoroughly enjoyed the beautiful views of the foothills and the friendly riders that we met along the way.

The history of Chatfield State Park reads just like the history of Cherry Creek State Park with both claiming to be the site for the first lumber industry and the initial purebred cattle industry. We do know that Civil War Lieutenant Isaac W. Chatfield bought 720 acres of land where Plum Creek and the South Platte river meet in 1870. He lived on and farmed the land for seven years. The U.S. Army Corps constructed the dam in 1967 to solve the recurring flooding problem in the area. The area around the reservoir became a state park in 1976.

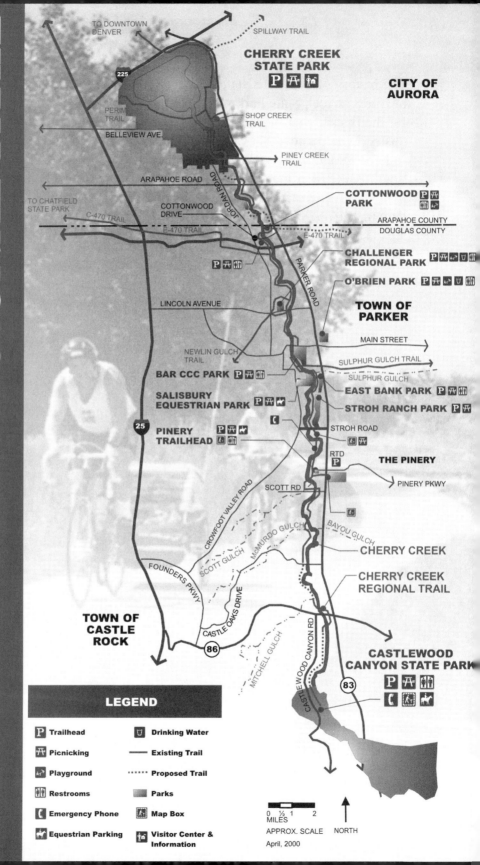

CHERRY CREEK REGIONAL TRAIL

TO DOWNTOWN DENVER

SPILLWAY TRAIL

CHERRY CREEK STATE PARK

CITY OF AURORA

225

PERIMETER TRAIL

SHOP CREEK TRAIL

BELLEVIEW AVE.

PINEY CREEK TRAIL

ARAPAHOE ROAD

JORDAN ROAD

COTTONWOOD PARK

TO CHATFIELD STATE PARK

C-470 TRAIL

COTTONWOOD DRIVE

E-470 TRAIL

E-470 TRAIL

ARAPAHOE COUNTY
DOUGLAS COUNTY

CHALLENGER REGIONAL PARK

PARKER ROAD

O'BRIEN PARK

LINCOLN AVENUE

TOWN OF PARKER

MAIN STREET

SULPHUR GULCH TRAIL

NEWLIN GULCH TRAIL

SULPHUR GULCH

BAR CCC PARK

EAST BANK PARK

SALISBURY EQUESTRIAN PARK

STROH RANCH PARK

STROH ROAD

PINERY TRAILHEAD

25

RTD
P

THE PINERY

SCOTT RD

PINERY PKWY

CROWFOOT VALLEY ROAD

SCOTT GULCH

McMURDO GULCH

BAYOU GULCH

CHERRY CREEK

FOUNDERS PKWY

CASTLE OAKS DRIVE

CHERRY CREEK REGIONAL TRAIL

MITCHELL GULCH

TOWN OF CASTLE ROCK

86

CASTLEWOOD CANYON RD

CASTLEWOOD CANYON STATE PARK

83

LEGEND

- P Trailhead
- Picnicking
- Playground
- Restrooms
- Emergency Phone
- Equestrian Parking
- Drinking Water
- — Existing Trail
- ······ Proposed Trail
- Parks
- Map Box
- Visitor Center & Information

0 ⅓ 1   2
MILES

APPROX. SCALE

NORTH

April, 2000

Cherry Creek Trailhead at North Pinery Parkway - Douglas County

Travel Distance: 12.9 miles
Time: 15 minutes
Travel Directions: Go east on Lincoln Avenue for 5.5 miles to Parker Road. Go south on Parker road for 6.6 miles to North Pinery Parkway (there is a light.) Stay in the right lane. Go west on North Pinery Parkway for 0.2 miles. Turn left into the parking lot.

Trailer Parking: The gravel parking lot has spaces for 4 or 5 trailers around the outer edges. Covered picnic area.
Fees: None
Water: No. However, horses can drink from the creek.
Restrooms: Yes, outhouse
Length of Ride: You can ride as long as you want going either north to Cottonwood (plans call for the trail to reach all the way to Cherry Creek State Park) or south to Highway 86 in Franktown, or both! This will be a 24 mile stretch of trail

when the plans are completed. Currently, there are 18.7 miles of trail ready for use.

Hazards: Walkers, bikers, dogs on leashes, bridges and water crossings and tunnels under roads. The park people prefer that horses use the water crossings but I found that some of these are very steep and soft so I used some of the bridges. This is an urban trail, especially going north, so you can get everything from construction to ambulances, paintball guns to soccer games.

Description of our ride: From the parking lot, we went through the gate and rode a short distance west to where it connects with the Cherry Creek Trail. Here we chose to ride south. We rode beside the paved bike path, crossed the creek and continued on for 0.5 miles. At this point, there is a gate at Scott Road. After going through the gate, we followed the signs which directed us to the left. We rode along Scott Road for 0.4 miles. This included crossing a very dilapidated bridge. Many of the old nails are risen and some of the planks are rotten. I found the north side of the bridge to be in the best condition. Since this bridge is used for vehicle traffic, I assume it is safe for us. Scott Road is a lightly used dirt road at this writing. After 0.4 miles, we followed the signs which directed us south onto Szymenski Road. We rode for 0.5 miles to a neighborhood recreation center. The trail remains dirt and goes to the east and back along the creek. Initially, we were riding close to back yards but soon we were in a wide open space between two neighborhoods. This part of the trail currently goes for 1.7 miles to Castle Oaks Drive. In 2004, the trail was completed to Highway 86 in Franktown. If you want to go that far, go right 0.25 miles when you reach Castle Oaks Drive. Then , you will need to go left back onto the trail. The trail is another 2 miles in length to Hwy. 86. In 2005 there will be great riding added on Hidden Mesa. The trail will connect 0.5 miles south of Castle Oaks Drive. It will go west onto the mesa or east to a new trailhead along Parker Road (Hwy. 83.) This will be called Hidden Mesa Trail.

From the North Pinery Parkway Trailhead, the Cherry Creek Trail is maintained by Douglas County Parks and Trails. North of Stroh Road, the trail is maintained by the Town of Parker. The plan is to connect Cherry Creek State Park with Castlewood Canyon. At this writing, the trail goes all the way north to the Douglas/Arapahoe County line and south to Franktown. Most of the time, you are riding beside the bike trail on a dirt path. It is easy going, mostly level and shoes are not required. The farther north that you go, the more urban the trail becomes, with more activity and traffic. They have built underpasses so you don't have to cross busy streets. This is a great conditioning trail and helps horses get used to seeing lots of new things while in a protected place. This is a fun trail to ride in the winter when the mountains are under snow.

Other trailheads currently include: Salisbury Equestrian Park, East Bank Trailhead and Cottonwood Trailhead, all maintained by the Town of Parker.

Columbine Open Space

Douglas County
Open Space &
Natural Resources

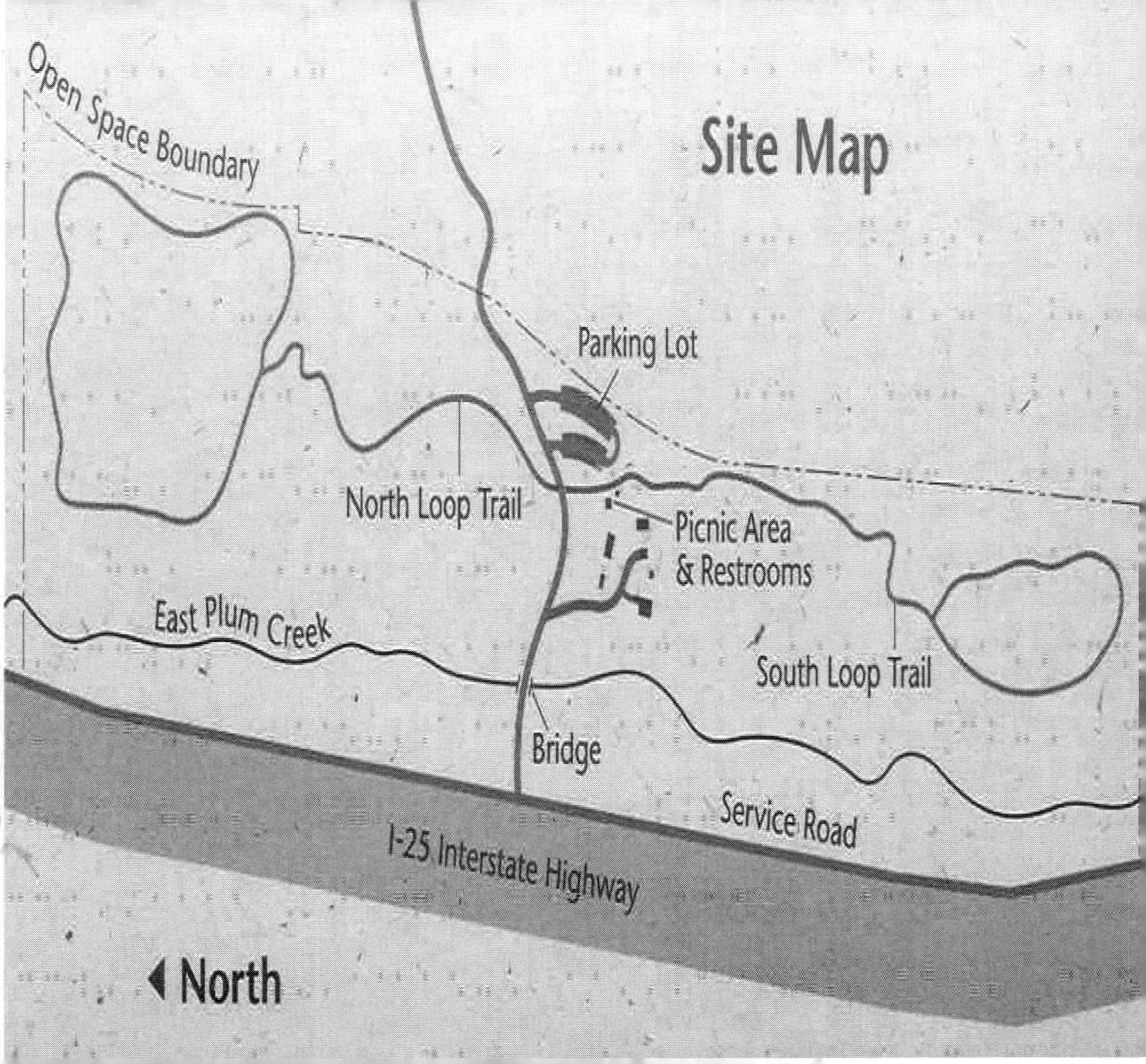

Site Map

- Open Space Boundary
- Parking Lot
- North Loop Trail
- Picnic Area & Restrooms
- South Loop Trail
- East Plum Creek
- Bridge
- Service Road
- I-25 Interstate Highway

◄ North

Columbine Open Space - Douglas County

Travel Distance: 18.5 miles
Travel Time: 20 minutes
Travel Directions: Go south on I-25 for 12.2 miles to exit #181, the Plum Creek Exit. At the stoplight at the end of the exit, turn left and go under the freeway for 0.2 miles. At the light turn right onto Wilcox which becomes the frontage road and drive for 6.1 miles. Columbine Open Space is on your left.

Trailer Parking: There is a large, drive-through, gravel parking lot that would hold 6-8 trailers if you use the upper loop parking area as well. Picnic tables and a Bar-B-Q are also available.
Fees: none
Water: Yes in the summer
Restrooms: Yes
Length of Ride: 3 miles - there are two loops, one to the south, one to the north. Both can be done at a nice leisurely walk or at a trot/canter pace. There is an additional 8 foot wide, crushed

concrete trail to the south that you can also ride.

Hazards: Hikers, bikers, wildlife, the freeway is visible on your west side and there is a train track on your east side. Dogs are not allowed in the Open Space as it is a protected wildlife area.

This area was opened in 1997 and currently only has a short trail. It took us about 25 minutes to walk the south loop and about 40 minutes to walk the north loop. It is a very pleasant trail even though you know you are not in the wilderness. There are lovely views of the front range. This is a great beginner's trail or a trail for a horse that is not in good condition. We used it for a trail to bring a new young horse on. The footing is very good and you would not need shoes.

Columbine Open Space is part of a 30,000 acre conservation corridor project that is designed to protect open space and wildlife habitat along this section of I-25.

Glendale Farm Open Space - Douglas County

Travel Distance: 3.3 miles
Travel Time: 6 minutes
Travel Directions: Go south on I-25 for 3.1 miles to exit #156 A, the Surrey Ridge exit. Be careful! It is a very sharp turn off the freeway. Turn left and proceed to the stop sign. Turn left and go under the freeway. The Open Space entrance is on your right.

Trailer Parking: Gravel parking lot but without designated trailer parking. It is not a big parking lot and could only hold 4 or 5 trailers if there were not a lot of cars there. Picnic table, benches, hitching post and call box are also available.
Fees: none
Water: No...A water pump from the old homestead did not work.
Restrooms: Yes, outhouse
Length of Ride: Short, 1.6 miles.

Hazards: Hikers, bikers, dogs on leashes, wildlife.

Description of our ride: This is a new open space and currently only has a short trail. It took us about 25 minutes to walk and trot a counterclockwise loop including a side trip to a view point. The views of the eastern prairies are beautiful. You also have views of the front range. There are several benches and hitching posts along the loop. The trail is single-lane and dirt. It goes up a gentle hill, along the east side of the open space, and back down. Shoes would not be needed. This is a great first trail for a young, or out-of-condition horse. We didn't come across any of the potential hazards on a weekday.

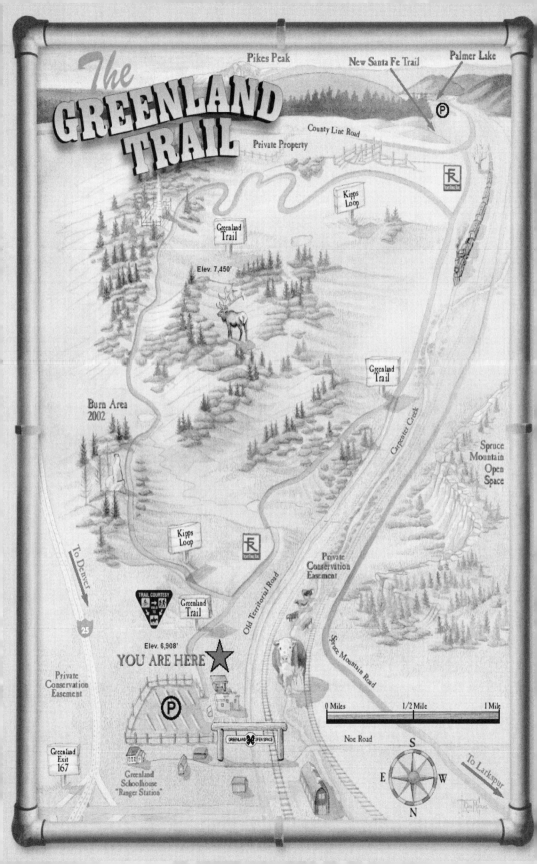

Greenland Open Space-Douglas County

Travel Distance: 26.5 miles
Time: 30 minutes
Travel Directions: Go south on I-25 for 25.6 miles. Take exit #167, the Greenland exit. At the bottom of exit, go west 0.25 miles then turn south 0.5 miles. The entrance is well marked with a beautiful sign.

Trailer Parking: There is a large gravel trailer parking lot next to a lovely covered area for picnicking at the trailhead. Douglas County Parks and Open Space Department asks that large groups call ahead so they arrange for overflow parking.
Fees: None
Water: Yes

Restroom: Yes, large port-a-potty, very clean.
Length of Ride: The loop within the park is 8.2 miles. We added on a ride to Palmer lake so our total ride was 10 miles.
Hazards: Several wide, dirt-covered culverts over washes along the Old Territorial Road. A train track runs parallel to the Old Territorial Road. If going on to Palmer Lake, there is a one foot high wooden rail to step over. Used by bicyclists, hikers and dogs on leashes.

Description of our trail ride: This is a new trail that is wide, well marked, and covered with finely crushed granite. Shoes would not be required and less-conditioned horses would do fine. It goes up and down gentle grasslands. We left the parking lot and rode south for 0.9 miles. At the trail junction, we turned left and proceeded up a hill and over a pine and scrub oak covered ridge. The views of the valley were beautiful. Up on the ridge are three lovely picnic sites with tables and hitching posts. We also came across a very old grave stone surrounded by a wrought iron fence. This little cemetery contains eight unmarked graves and a large marble stone marking the grave of Edward Thomas Kipps who, as the stone said, "is not dead but sleeping." We followed the trail back down to where it connects with the western part of the loop. At this point, we turned south and rode out of the open space, across County Line Road, and onto a new trail that leads to Palmer Lake in El Paso County. This trail took us to the trailhead of the New Santa Fe Trail that leads all the way down to the Air Force Academy. Here we stopped for lunch at the park by the lake. It has a wonderful new restroom with running water! We rode back to the parking lot by the lower, westerly part of the loop. Part of this loop goes along the Old Territorial Road which runs parallel to, but not right next to, a train track. We discovered that, at least on this day, a very long freight train uses that track at 1:35 p.m. My horse was the only one upset by the train so I was glad I wasn't alone at the time. Speaking of alone, we only saw two hikers the whole day. Our guess is that this is a well-used open space during warmer times of the year and on weekends. So, while this is a close-in open space, be aware that solo riders may truly be solo! I am sure this beautiful open space will be used more and more as it gets discovered. This was a wonderful ride that could be done at a leisurely pace or at a fast pace for conditioning.

In 1994, Douglas County Citizens voted to fund Douglas County Open Space projects. This beautiful open space is one of the results. It was officially opened in June of 2003. The name of Greenland was penned by Helen Hunt Jackson, an author and poet. The little community of Greenland was founded along the Denver and Rio Grande Railroads around 1871. The beautiful red barn close to the trailhead is part of the Greenland Ranch which was homesteaded in the early 1870's.

Beautiful map courtesy of Douglas County Division of Open Space and Natural Resources.

Highline Canal Trailhead - Douglas County

Travel Distance: 20.1 miles
Travel Time: 28 minutes
Travel Directions: Go north on I-25 for 0.9 miles to the C-470 exit. Take C-470 west for 9.3 miles to the Santa Fe (Hwy. 85) exit. At the light at the end of the exit ramp, turn left onto Santa Fe. Drive for 3.9 miles to the Titan Parkway exit ramp. At the top of the ramp turn right (west) and drive for 2.5 miles to Roxborough Park Road. Turn right and drive for 1.6 miles. The trailhead is on your right.

Trailer Parking: A large circular gravel parking lot that will hold 4 to 6 trailers parked along the sides. Beautiful covered picnic table area.
Fees: none
Water: No
Restrooms: Yes, Port-A-Potty
Length of Ride: We rode for 3 hours
Hazards: Joggers, remote control airplanes from Chatfield

State Park, water crossings to the east, Titan Road crossing and gates going west.

Description of our ride: This is a new trailhead and was just opened in the summer of 2004. It provides wonderful access to the Douglas County section of the Highline Canal. You could do two different rides from this location. If you ride to the east, the wide sandy canal trail ends at the south east corner of Chatfield State Park where the canal goes underground. Here you turn into the park on a single lane dirt trail. This trail weaves through the trees along Plum Creek. We had fun jumping logs along here. You can ride as far as you want just staying on the trails in the park as there are 24 miles of trails in Chatfield State Park that are available for equestrian use. This section of the park is not used as heavily as other parts of the park so it is a very pleasant place to spend the day.

A second day you can go to the west along the canal trail. It will take you along the south side of Chatfield State Park and you will have to deal with wayward remote control airplanes which were very scary to our horses. Once you get past that, you have a wonderful, wide, sandy trail that will take you for five miles to the Waterton Canyon parking lot. To get that far, you will pass Cottonwood Riding Club and cross Titan Road. After crossing Titan road, you will have to go through some gates. You will be riding beside the canal and along the back-yards of homes and beside farms. Some of these areas close to Chatfield are slated for development so you will have construction to deal with in the future. This trail is flat and sandy. It is a great place for conditioning and shoes are not necessary. This is a great year-round trail.

Indian Creek Equestrian Trail

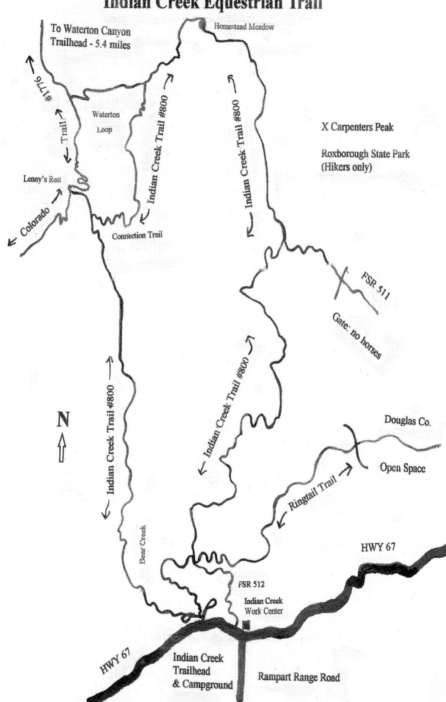

To Waterton Canyon
Trailhead - 5.4 miles

Homestead Meadow

Trail #1776

Waterton
Loop

Indian Creek Trail #800

Indian Creek Trail #800

X Carpenters Peak

Roxborough State Park
(Hikers only)

Lenny's Rest

Colorado

Connection Trail

FSR 511

Gate: no horses

Indian Creek Trail #800

Indian Creek Trail #800

N

Douglas Co.

Open Space

Ringtail Trail

HWY 67

Bear Creek

FSR 512

Indian Creek
Work Center

HWY 67

Indian Creek
Trailhead
& Campground

Rampart Range Road

Indian Creek - Douglas County

Travel Distance: 21.5 miles
Travel Time: 35 minutes
Travel Directions: Go south on I-25 for 5.7 miles to Exit #187, Happy Canyon Road. At the top of the exit ramp, turn right onto Happy Canyon and curve down the hill for 2.2 miles to Hwy. 85. Turn right and drive for 3.2 miles to the light at SH 67 and turn left into the town of Sedalia. Go south on SH 67 for 10.4 miles past Rampart Range Road to the trailhead on your right.

Trailer Parking: A large gravel parking lot that will hold 6 or more trailers. Easy, straight, drive-through.
Fees: Yes, $4.00
Water: Yes but turned off in the winter.
Restrooms: Yes, outhouse
Length of Ride: We made a 6 mile loop. However, this trail connects to many other trails including the Colorado Trail so you could ride for days!

Hazards: Water Crossings, some rocky places, some steep drop-offs, winter damage always leaves some trees across the trail that may not be cleared away until summer, step over rail by the outhouse to get onto the trail, hikers, dogs on leashes, bikers.

Description of our ride: We have ridden the trails at Indian Creek many times from short trips to the entire loop. We have also ridden the trail to Waterton Canyon. The official Indian Creek Trail #800 is a 14 mile loop and takes the whole day. On the day that we went on the "test ride" for this book, we stepped over the rail by the outhouse and took an immediate right onto the Indian Creek Trail. As we rode up the trail, we were treated to some beautiful views of Devil's Head and the surrounding forest. At the top of the ridge, there are several trails going in different directions. Here the new Ringtail Trail joins in from Sharptail Ridge. You must choose which way you want to go. We followed the Indian Creek trail to the left which was an old forest service road at this point. We followed this dirt road for several miles going north. You will pass other "unofficial" trails going off of this one. The trails are not clearly marked so we need to get an eagle scout out there to put up signs to mark the Indian Creek Trail.

On another ride, we went west from the parking lot through the equestrian camp ground to the western side of the Indian Creek Trail. You will cross Bear Creek a couple of times and ride across the tops of ridges. Lenny's Rest is a bench that is a great lunch stop.

This is one of our favorite trails, especially in the summer as it always seems to be a pleasant temperature when it is hot everywhere else. It is also one of the best fall rides as the scrub oak are beautiful.

Camping at Indian Creek will cost you $14.00 per night. Make reservations by calling 877-444-6777.

69

Salisbury Equestrian Park
Cherry Creek Trail - Douglas County

Travel Distance: 7.4 miles
Travel Time: 12 minutes
Travel Directions: Go east on Lincoln for 4.1 miles. Turn right onto Jordon Road. Drive south on Jordon Road for 1.2 miles to Mainstreet. Turn left onto Mainstreet and drive for 0.4 miles to Motsenbocker Road. Turn right and follow Motsenbocker for 1.5 miles. The park entrance is on your left by the Parker Public Works office.

Trailer Parking: Upon entering the park it was difficult to determine where the trailers were supposed to park. There was an open area to our left next the rodeo arena but there was a sign that said "No Horses." So, we drove along the dirt road that borders what was once the polo field and parked on the east side by the outdoor riding arena.
Fees: None
Water: Yes, over by the baseball diamonds or back by the Public Works office.
Restroom: Yes

Length of Ride: We rode north for 3 miles then turned back for a total of 6 miles.

Hazards: This trail has become a very urban trail so you must be prepared for anything. On the day we test-rode it, we interrupted a paint-ball war in the area that was once the carriage-driving obstacle course. There is a lot of construction of homes going on along many parts of the trail. Much of the equestrian trail runs beside the bike path which is used by bicyclists, rollerbladers, walkers, joggers and dogs on leashes. There are also water crossings, bridges and crossings that go under busy roads.

Description of our ride: We parked and tacked up beside a very nice outdoor arena. The arena has nice sandy footing and dressage letters around it. We rode around the lake just south of the arena then rode north toward the old, now neglected, driving obstacle course. Coming down the hill, we came across a paintball war being waged between seven teenage boys. This was frightening for the horses but the boys stopped as soon as they saw us. We crossed the wooden covered bridge and followed the trail north and east until it joined with the Cherry Creek Trail. We rode up to the Bar Triple C Park area. Here there is a nice picnic area with a covered picnic table and outhouses. We continued north and rode under the Mainstreet overpasses. This was a bit frightening for the horses both with the noise of the cars and trucks overhead and the moving shadows. We continued along the sandy, clearly marked trail up to the Parker Recreation Center by Lincoln before turning around and returning to the Park. The Cherry Creek Trail continues North to the Douglas County/Arapaho County Line and south to Hwy. 86 in Franktown. Shoes would not be necessary and this would be a good schooling trail to help your horse get used to anything! It is very flat so horses do not need to be in great shape.

Note: Salisbury Equestrian Park can also be accessed from the east side of the creek at the East Bank Trailhead along Parker Road. However, there is no designated trailer parking at that site though there is usually plenty of room.

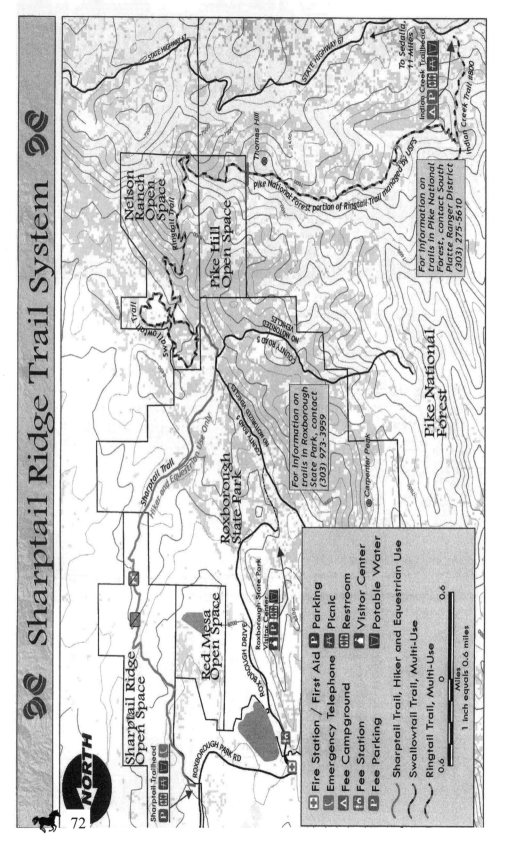

Sharptail Ridge Trail System

NORTH

72

Sharptail Ridge Open Space

Sharptail Trailhead

ROXBOROUGH PARK RD

Red Mesa Open Space

ROXBOROUGH DRIVE

Roxborough State Park
Visitor Center

Roxborough State Park

COUNTY ROAD 5
NO MOTORIZED VEHICLES

Sharptail Trail
Hiker and Equestrian Use Only

For information on trails in Roxborough State Park, contact (303) 973-3959

Swallowtail Trail

COUNTY ROAD 5
NO MOTORIZED VEHICLES

Nelson Ranch Open Space

Ringtail Trail

Pike Hill Open Space

Pike National Forest portion of Ringtail Trail managed by USFS

Thomas Hill

STATE HIGHWAY 67

STATE HIGHWAY 67

To Sedalia, 11 Miles

Indian Creek Trailhead

Indian Creek Trail #800

For information on trails in Pike National Forest, contact South Platte Ranger District (303) 275-5610

Pike National Forest

Carpenter Peak

Legend

- ✚ Fire Station / First Aid
- ✆ Emergency Telephone
- ⛺ Fee Campground
- 🏠 Fee Station
- P Fee Parking

- P Parking
- 🍴 Picnic
- 🚻 Restroom
- 👁 Visitor Center
- ▽ Potable Water

~ Sharptail Trail, Hiker and Equestrian Use
~ Swallowtail Trail, Multi-Use
~ Ringtail Trail, Multi-Use

Miles
0.6   0   0.6
1 inch equals 0.6 miles

Sharptail Ridge Open Space - Douglas County

Travel Distance: 20.1 miles
Travel Time: 28 minutes
Travel Directions: Go north on I-25 for 0.9 miles to the C-470 exit. Take C-470 west for 9.3 miles to the Santa Fe (Hwy. 85) exit. At the light at the end of the exit ramp, turn left onto Santa Fe. Drive for 3.9 miles to the Titan Parkway exit ramp. At the top of the ramp turn right (west) and drive for 2.5 miles to Roxborough Park Road. Turn left and drive for 3.5 miles to the open space entrance on your left.

Trailer Parking: A large circular gravel parking lot that will hold 6 or more trailers parked along the sides. Beautiful covered picnic table area. Douglas County Parks and Open Space Department recommends that large groups call ahead so they can arrange for over-flow parking.
Fees: none
Water: Yes

Restrooms: Yes, Port-A-Potty

Length of Ride: The trail weaves south for 4.4 miles. In addition, you can leave the open space at this point and ride a 3.5 mile loop or go even farther by riding all the way to Indian Creek Trail and the trails that connect to it. (See Indian Creek Trail write up.)

Hazards: Hikers and equestrians are the only ones allowed to use this area. No dogs are allowed. If you go onto County Road 5 at the south, you will have a step-over rail to get back into the open space. You must resist the temptation to gallop across the rolling prairie, however, as your greatest hazard could be getting a ticket and a fine for not staying on the trail! This is a designated wildlife and natural area. When we rode this trail in February we were treated to a viewing of elk and deer. We are lucky to be able to ride here.

Description of our ride: This is a new trail and was just dedicated in the summer of 2004. The first time we rode it, the trail was nothing more that a four foot wide strip of mowed grass. You are not allowed to ride on the two-tire track maintenance road. When we rode it a second time during the winter of 2005, the trail was well defined and packed dirt. As you ride over the rolling hills, you will have beautiful views of the red rocks in Roxborough State Park. During our winter ride, we saw a large herd of elk. We rode for 4 easy miles to County Road 5. Here riders can turn around and go back or continue on. If you choose to go on, you will ride onto County Road 5. Go left on the dirt road. In a few yards, step over the rail onto the last 0.3 miles of Sharptail Trail. This area is actually part of Roxborough State Park. The first time we entered this section of the trail, there was a sign posted which read: "3.5 mile double loop and return here, 2.5 miles just upper loop and return, 0.7 mi. to Ringtail Trail cut off to NF." When we returned in the winter the sign was gone. When you pass a green gate, you will be on the Nelson Ranch Open Space and the Swallowtail Trail. This trail is named after the Tiger Swallowtail butterfly so be on the lookout for them. There are 2 beautiful new picnic tables and hitching posts along this trail for lunch stops. An Eagle Scout also built 6 benches along the way. The Swallowtail Trail has some rocky sections. If you follow this trail just over a quarter mile from the green gate, the trail will connect with the Ringtail Trail which will take you all the way up to the trails in Pike National Forest. You can ride to Waterton Canyon Dam by way of the Indian Creek Trail. The Indian Creek Trail can also connect you to the Colorado Trail. This section is much more forested as it begins the climb up to the Indian Creek Trail. We rode for 9 miles, 4.5 miles out and then back and it took us 3.5 hours. This is a very pleasant ride and great for beginning riders and horses as well as a great place to condition. Shoes would not be required but are a good idea if you want to go up into the National Forest land.

NOTE: Sharptail Ridge Open Space is closed for big game hunting season during part of September and October so call Douglas County Open Space and Natural Resources Department at 303-660-7495 for the exact dates.

Map courtesy of Douglas County Division of Open Space and Natural Resources.

Waterton Canyon-Pike National Forest-Douglas County

Travel Distance: 15.5 miles
Travel Time: 18 minutes
Travel Directions: Go north on I-25 for just under a mile to the C-470 west exit. Drive 12.1 miles west on C-470 to the Wadsworth exit. At the bottom of the exit, turn left onto Wadsworth. Travel 4.4 miles to Waterton Road. Turn left onto Waterton Road and drive for 0.3 miles to the Kassler Water Treatment Plant. There is a large parking lot on your left across the street from the water plant.

Trailer Parking: A large dirt and gravel lot is available for many trailers. Follow the signs to the right side.
Fees: none
Water: There are places along the canyon where horses can drink from the South Platte River.
Restroom: Yes, outhouse

 76

Length of Ride: 12 miles from Kassler to Strontia Dam and back.

Hazards: Hikers, bikers, lots of fishermen, wildlife, the noise from the water coming out of the dam may frighten some horses, step-over rail at the start of the trail, you must cross Waterton Road to get to the trail and it has become a busy two-lane road, bridge right after crossing road, big horn sheep herd in canyon, no dogs are allowed.

Description of our ride: The 6 miles up to Strontia Dam is on a wide gravel service road. There are some side areas frequented by picnickers or fishermen that you can ride along as well. This road is nearly flat all the way to the dam. If your horse is shod you can trot or canter but my barefoot horse didn't like the small, sharp gravel. You must also beware of bikers and hikers. This is a heavily used trail. One of the days we were there, the herd of big horn sheep that lives on the cliffs along the canyon put on quite a show for us, from climbing up the sides of the cliffs to butting heads. The horses were not impressed! At the top by the dam there is a very nice picnic area. The roar and mist from the dam is scary for the horses, however.

On another ride, we came to Waterton Canyon from the Indian Creek Trailhead by getting on the Colorado Trail and going north.

This is a good place to come with your non-horsy family members. While you ride, they can bike or fish.

Fun Fact: Did you know that the Strontia Springs Dam was used in the filming of one of the Superman movies?

77

RIDING COLORADO

EL PASO COUNTY

Maps developed for this book by Brian Kay at El Paso County Parks Department.

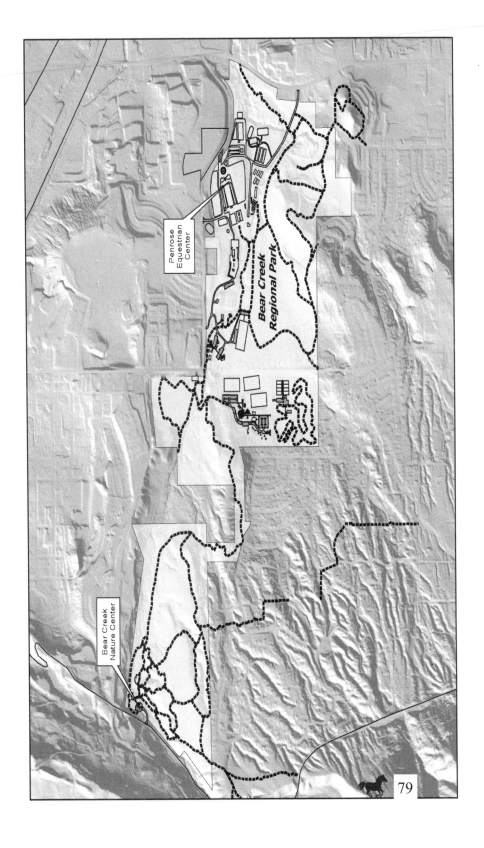

Penrose
Equestrian
Center

*Bear Creek
Regional Park*

Bear Creek
Nature Center

79

Bear Creek Regional Park-El Paso County

Travel Distance: 53.6 miles
Travel Time: 1 hour
Travel Directions: Go south on I-25 for 52.5 miles to Hwy. 24 (exit # 141 - Cimarron St.) Go west on Hwy. 24 for 0.3 miles to the first light which is 8th Street. Turn left on 8th Street and drive south for 0.4 miles to the light at Rio Grande. Turn right and drive up the hill. Penrose Equestrian Center is 0.4 miles up on your left.

Trailer Parking: Upon entering the Penrose property, you can either go down the hill toward the show barns and park in the huge gravel area just past the barns, or you may park to your right over by the office buildings. If there is a large show going on you would be better off driving farther up Rio Grande to the Park Headquarters where you can park in the gravel lot by the community gardens.
Fees: None
Water: Yes
Restroom: Yes. If the show facility is locked, you can use the restrooms up the hill at the office.
Length of Ride: 2.5 hours.
Hazards: Joggers, cyclists, baby strollers and playground, road crossings, bridges, dogs on leashes, wildlife.

Description of our ride: We chose to come to this trail on a beautiful, dry December day. We were all rejoicing about living in Colorado and having such fabulous winter days to ride. We parked down the hill by the show barns in the huge gravel lot. We started our ride at the east end of the park and picked various trails that weave around the cross-country jump course. We eventually ended up by the Park Headquarters which is on the corner of Rio Grande and 21st Street. At this point, we rode past a playground which the 4 year old I was riding did not like one bit! We managed to get by that obstacle and pushed the crosswalk button at 21st. We crossed the road and entered the

 80

western section of the park. This part of the park seems a little more remote even though you are still close to civilization. We saw more wildlife and fewer people. The trail climbs gently as you ride west. Since we had several hours, we crossed Bear Creek Road and Upper Gold Camp Road and got on the Red Rock Loop Trail in Manitou Section 16 Park. We climbed up a ridge, then took a right onto the Red Rock Meadow Trail where we found a lovely spot to stop and have lunch.

The Bear Creek Regional Park trail is a very easy trail. There are 10 miles of trails just within this park. It is soft dirt or sand so shoes would not be necessary. The scenery is beautiful with views of the city and Red Rocks Park. It would be a wonderful fall ride when the scrub oak are red. As you go west, the trail climbs gently in elevation. If you choose to continue on into Manitou Section 16 you are in for a much different ride and shoes would be recommended. It gets steep and rocky the farther you go. You can also connect to the Bear Creek Park that is maintained by the City of Colorado Springs.

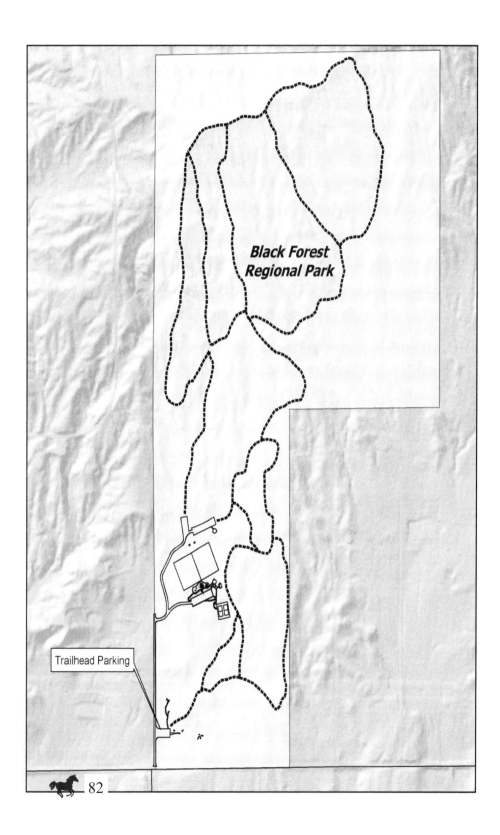

**Black Forest
Regional Park**

Trailhead Parking

Black Forest Regional Park - El Paso County

Travel Distance: 47 miles
Travel Time: 48 minutes
Travel Directions: Go south on I-25 for 33 miles to exit 161, the Monument Exit. At the end of the exit, go right (east) for 5.2 miles to Hwy. 83. Turn right onto 83 and go 6.7 miles to Shoup Road. Go left onto Shoup Road for 2.2 miles. Go left onto Milam Road and right into the parking lot. If this lot is full you may go on up Milam Rd to the next parking lot and park in the back section of the main parking area.

Trailer Parking: The first parking lot will hold about 4 trailers if there are no cars in the way. The other lot is a bit bigger. Both are dirt. There are picnic tables.
Fees: none
Water: Only up by the main picnic area.
Restrooms: Only up by the main picnic area.
Length of Ride: We had a lovely 2 hour ride.

Hazards: Hikers, bikers, dogs on leashes.

Description of our ride: This park is like a little brother to Fox Run. It has the same feel but without the beautiful lake area. The trails are well maintained and weave around through the ponderosa pine forest for which the Black Forest is known. We immediately set off up the hill to find the re-strooms and then began exploring the park. The trails criss-cross the park in lots of circular loops. You can ride around for a couple of hours without repeating yourself. None of the trails were labeled but you won't have trouble finding your way back to your trailer as the park is not that big and the un-derbrush is kept cleared out. You will do a little up

and down of hills but nothing major. At the top of some of the hills you will get a beautiful view of Pikes Peak. This is a very easy and beautiful trail. It is a good beginner's trail ride or a great place to condition your horse. Shoes would not be neces-sary.

This trail might be difficult in the winter if snow is on the ground as the trees would create shade and the sand on the trails would melt the snow just enough to create ice patches. This is what we encountered at Fox Run during the winter. It would be a fabulous summer, spring or fall ride!

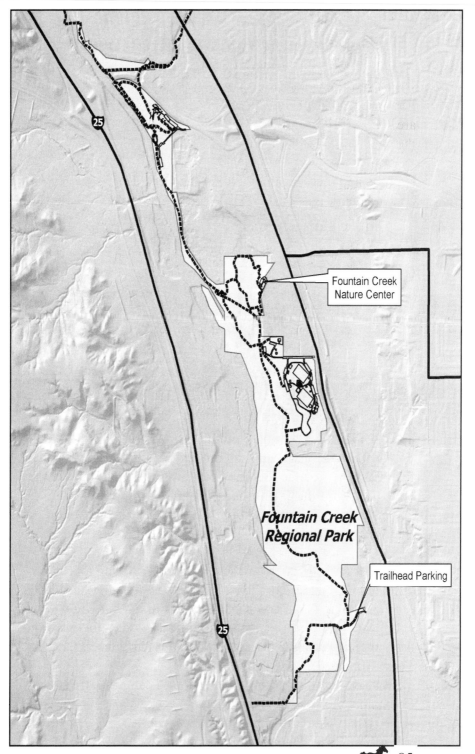

Fountain Creek
Nature Center

Fountain Creek
Regional Park

Trailhead Parking

85

Fountain Creek Regional Trail
El Paso County

Travel Distance: 62.7 miles
Travel Time: 1 hour and 5 minutes
Travel Directions: From Lincoln and I-25 drive south on I-25 for 61.6 miles to exit 132, the Fountain Exit. Go left on Hwy. 16 at the top of the exit for 0.7 miles. Go right on Hwy. 85 and take an immediate right onto Willow Springs Road for 0.4 miles.

Trailer Parking: There are several gravel parking lots at the trailhead. We parked in the end one as the others were closed for the winter. There was room for 3-4 trailers but you need to get in early before cars block your turn-around as there was no drive through access or designated trailer parking.
Fees: None
Water: Not at this parking lot but horses can drink from Fountain Creek.
Restrooms: Not at this parking lot
Length of Ride: Down and back on the existing trail is 7

 86

miles. We took it easy as we had a young horse with us so our ride lasted 2.5 hours.

Hazards: This trail has some of the typical urban trail hazards. We came across some construction work using a backhoe. There is a train track visible to the east. You will also encounter bikers, hikers, dogs on leashes, and bridges over river crossings. The duck viewing shelters must have looked like caves to the horses because they were all scared of them. You pass a sewage treatment plant, a noisy waterfall and ducks that take flight unexpectedly!

Description of our ride: I know that that sounds like a lot of hazards but this is really a wonderful place to ride! From the parking lot we followed the trail south. This is a flat trail that is wide enough for three abreast. It is packed sand and great to ride on. When we came to the waterfall, we had a few skittish horses but

no big problems. The trail continues to follow along Fountain Creek, past the other trailheads and across a large bridge until it ends

at private property. This was really a pleasant place to ride and would be a wonderful winter ride on one of our infamous bright, sunny, winter days. It would also be a great trail for conditioning or ponying a second horse. No shoes would be required.

87

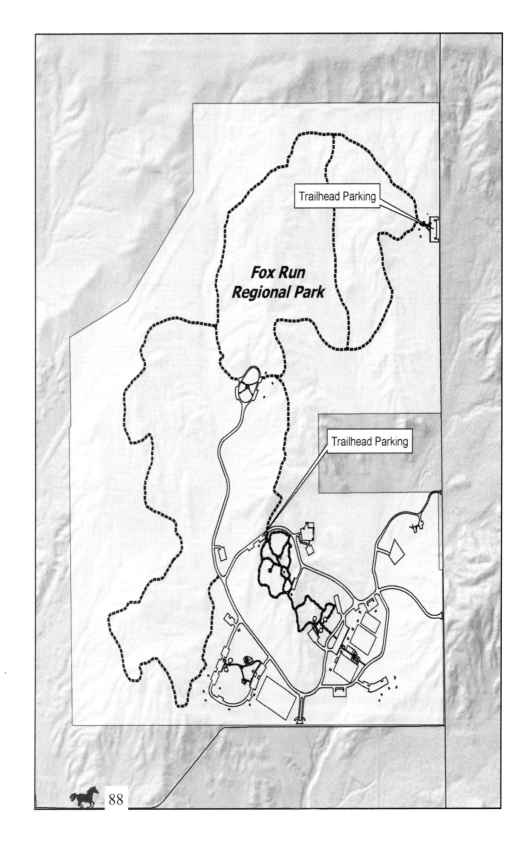

Trailhead Parking

Fox Run
Regional Park

Trailhead Parking

Fox Run Regional Park - El Paso County

Travel Distance: 43 miles
Travel Time: 46 minutes
Travel Directions: Go south on I-25 for 37.8 miles to exit 156 A. Be careful! It is a very sharp turn off the freeway. Drive 3.2 miles east on Northgate Road to Rollercoaster. Turn left on Rollercoaster and drive 1.5 miles to the small east entrance to the park on your left. Another entrance to the park is on the south off Stella Drive.

You may also get to the park by going south on Parker Road (Hwy. 83.) Turn right on Hwy.105 then left on Rollercoaster. Rollercoaster takes a little jog to the east on Higby Road.

Trailer Parking: Long gravel parking lot but without designated trailer parking. Picnic tables.
Fees: None
Water: Yes
Restrooms: Yes, very nice
Length of Ride: We had a lovely 2 hour ride.

Hazards: Hikers, bikers, dogs on leashes, short wooden bridges, wildlife. One trail on the west side goes through a tunnel under the road. In the winter, the sandy trails were extremely icy.

Description of our ride: Fox Run Regional Park is one of the most beautiful and well maintained parks I have ridden. The trails are wide sand and weave through thick ponderosa pines. The views of Pikes Peak are spectacular. There are lovely picnic areas throughout the park. The playground area is quite popular for families and group picnics but the riding trails are not crowded at all. The trails around the lakes are off-limits to horses but the road around the lake is available to you.

We visited this park in the fall and in the winter. From the trailhead, we just picked our trails as we went along, first heading west then south to the playground area then north up the hill to the lakes and back around to the parking lot. There are several loops that you can take within the trails we rode to lengthen your ride. When we went there during the winter, we had a terrible time negotiating the trails because they were so icy.  It seems that the sand radiates enough heat to melt the snow just enough to have it freeze into sheets of ice at night. This area tends to get a bit more snow than the surrounding area so be wary of riding it in the winter. Hilly trails would be good for conditioning and the surface of the trails would not require shoes.

Garden of the Gods - El Paso County

Travel Distance: 54.2 miles
Travel Time: 1 hour
Travel Directions: Go south on I-25 for 47.2 miles to exit 146, "Garden of the Gods Road." Go west on Garden of the Gods Road for 2.6 miles. Turn left at the light onto 30th Street and drive 1.5 miles to the park entrance on your right. Follow Gateway Road west for 0.4 miles. Go right on Juniper Way Loop for 2.2 miles. Turn left on Garden Lane toward the trading post for 0.3 miles to the parking lot on your left.

Trailer Parking: Designated trailer parking on the diagonal for 5 or 6 trailers. Paved lot, picnic tables.
Fees: None
Water: Not at the lot
Restrooms: Not at the lot. You will have to ride back to the trading post.
Length of Ride: 2.5 hours.

Hazards: Hikers, bikers, dogs on leashes, wildlife, road crossings within the park can be busy during the summer, small water crossings, some steep climbs to some of the rock formations. Some of the trails around the formations are solid rock.

Description of our ride: We began our ride by taking the Strusenback Trail across the street from the parking lot. We followed this trail to a service road, turned right and rode to the Hamp Hut. We went left on the Scotsman Trail to Buckskin Charley Trail. We crossed Ridge Road and followed Chambers Trail to Rock Ledge Ranch. After exploring the beautiful ranch, we stopped for lunch. We then followed the Susan Bretag Trail all the way north to where it connects with the Palmer Trail. The Palmer Trail takes you to the Siamese Twins rock formation and gives you beautiful views of the central garden part of the park. It is the prettiest section of trail. We then rode the Cabin Canyon Trail south past the trading post and back to the Spring Canyon Picnic area where the trailers were parked. The trails are usually packed dirt. Over by the Siamese Twins, you will encounter some rocky areas but not bad. Shoes would not be required.

I would recommend getting a trail map at the visitor's center when you get to the park as the trails, especially in the Scotsman Picnic Area, are very confusing and not always clearly marked. Horses are not allowed in the Central Garden area.

Garden of the Gods is one of the most beautiful areas you will ride in and is basically a year-round park. This is a city owned park which was given to the city of Colorado Springs in 1909 by the children of Charles Elliot Perkins as a result of his desire that it be kept as a park forever. What a gift to all of us!

Horses can be rented for trail rides through Garden of the Gods by contacting Academy Riding Stables at: 1-888-700-0410 or on line at www.academyridingstables.com.

 92

Gold Camp Road Trail, North Cheyenne Canyon Park-El Paso County

Travel Distance: 60 miles
Travel Time: 1 hour 15 minutes
Travel Directions: Go south on I-25 for 52.5 miles to Hwy. 24 (exit # 141 - Cimarron St.) Go west on Hwy. 24 for 1.5 miles. Turn left onto 21st Street and drive 0.8 miles to Lower Gold Camp Road. Turn right onto Lower Gold Camp Road and drive for 1.1 miles to Bear Creek Road (26th street.) Turn left. Travel for 0.9 miles on this winding road. At the stop sign, take a sharp left turn onto Gold Camp Road. After 2.2 miles, this becomes a very narrow dirt road with sharp blind

turns. Fortunately there is not much traffic but go slowly. Follow Gold Camp Road for a total of 3.9 miles to the parking lot above the Helen Hunt Falls. This will take you through two single- lane tunnels so go slowly. Another option is to stop at the trailhead at the 2.9 mile point and ride the last mile through the tunnels. On weekdays there is not a lot of traffic on the road. I would recommend stopping at the first parking lot if you have a very long trailer.

Trailer Parking: An open gravel area is available with plenty of room for many trailers.
Fees: none
Water: Not at trailhead but you can find spots along the stream.
Restroom: No
Length of Ride: 16 miles to complete the trail to Old Stage Road and back.
Hazards: Tunnels, hikers, wildlife, 1 small river crossing. This is a multi-use trail and is open to both mountain bikers and dirt bikes.

Description of our ride: This trail is an old railroad bed. In the 1890's a railroad carried gold ore from the mines in Cripple Creek to the smelter in Colorado Springs. The entire route was 25 miles long. It must have been a very busy track in its day as the mines at Cripple Creek yielded $5 to $10 Billion dollars worth of gold at today's prices. When the mines were no longer profitable, the tracks were torn up and it was made into a road. Fortunately for hikers, bikers and equestrians, tunnel #3 partially collapsed in 1988. This eliminated vehicle traffic on an eight mile section of the road. It has now become a wonderful multi-use trail. From the parking lot, you will ride up this wide sand and dirt road. When you come to tunnel #3, you will take a narrow dirt trail around and over it. You will then make a small water crossing over Buffalo Creek by taking the trail to the left and get back down to the road. After this, it is free sailing along a beautiful road. It makes a gentle climb as it goes around mountains and through tunnels. As you go through the tunnels, look up and see the black soot from the old trains. At 5.6 miles and 6 miles you will come to the Eureka Mine and the St. Peters Dome Mine. Both of these are favorite mineral collecting spots. The views of Cheyenne Mountain and Colorado Springs are fabulous and you will enjoy the Pikes Peak Granite rock formations with their pinkish color and characteristic rounded shapes.

The trail is wide with a gentle incline. After riding this trail, I took my husband and youngest child back for an "easy" bike ride. I soon discovered that the "gradual incline" is a lot harder when you are on a bicycle! It is great for conditioning and ponying a second horse. Shoes are not required.

If you desire to go onto Old Stage Road, know that vehicles are allowed from here on.

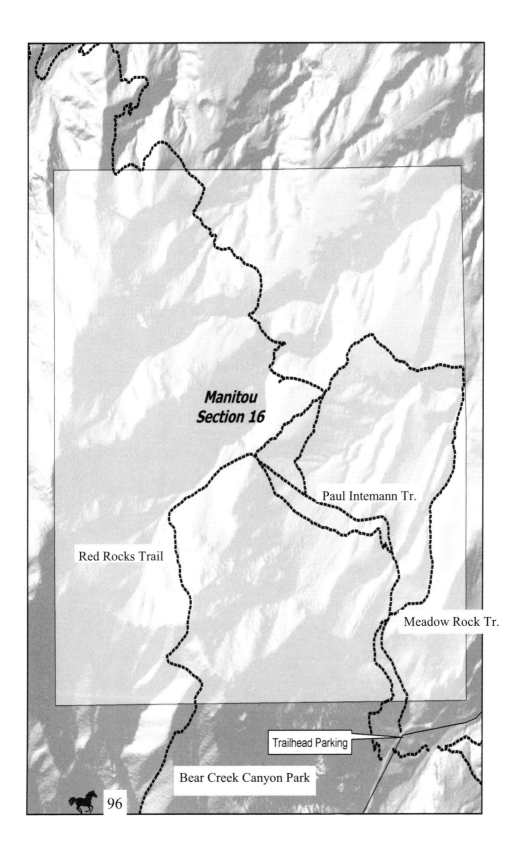

*Manitou
Section 16*

Paul Intemann Tr.

Red Rocks Trail

Meadow Rock Tr.

Trailhead Parking

Bear Creek Canyon Park

Manitou Section 16-El Paso County

Travel Distance: 60 miles

Travel Time: 1 hour 10 minutes

Travel Directions: Go south on I-25 for 52.5 miles from the Lincoln exit to Hwy. 24 (exit # 141 - Cimarron St.) Go west on Hwy. 24 for 1.5 miles. Turn left on 21st Street and drive 0.8 miles to Lower Gold Camp Road. Turn right on Lower Gold Camp Road and drive to the stop sign. Go straight, after stopping, onto Gold Camp Road. This is a total of 2.0 miles. Pass the first parking lot on the west side of the road. Proceed to the wide turn-around on your left just past a big water storage tank set low on the hill on your left.

Trailer Parking: The closest trailer parking to the trailhead is nothing more than a wide turnoff on the east side of Gold Camp Road. It will hold 3 trailers. Large groups would have to park down by the Parks Department (See Bear Creek Regional Park) and ride through Bear Creek Regional Park to get to this point.

Water: No

Restrooms: No

Length of Ride: The entire Red Rocks Trail from Manitou Section 16 into Bear Creek Canyon Park on the Palmer Trail (also called the Crystal Park Trail) and back along the road to the parking area is 6 miles. One and 1/2 miles of this is along High Drive which is a one way road.

Hazards: DO NOT ride the Paul Intemann loop that goes off to the right as you ride up the Red Rocks Trail. As it comes back up the hill to rejoin the Red Rocks Trail, you will get into a very narrow trail with steep sides and loose footing as well as very high rock ledges to climb up. As you get near to the top of the ridge on the Red Rocks Trail, you will come to one difficult section that is very steep and narrow with 3 switch backs. Here the rocks are loose and the footing is difficult. It is easier to go up this part than down. The trail is narrow and rocky in places. During the winter, water flows down the trail and freezes making it a sheet of ice. Hikers, dogs on leashes (or in our experience, *off* leashes,) mountain bikers, wildlife. To complete the loop, you will ride along High Drive which is a one-way, lightly used road.

Description of our ride: The first part of the trail is rather rocky but soon gets better. A short way up we came to a junction with the Meadow Rock Trail going to the right. We went down this narrow, dirt trail that winds through the trees until it reached the meadow at the bottom. At this point, you will see a fence with private property signs on it. We were afraid to cross it even though it appeared that the trail went there. To our left was a canyon where what appeared to be another trail was covered with ice. So, neither option looked good. There was a very narrow trail that went along the fence but too close for comfort. So, back we went to the Red Rocks Trail. The canyon trail looked like it might be interesting another day.

As you go up the Red Rocks Trail, you will see where the Paul Intemann Nature trail goes off to the right. This trail is still in the developmental stage and is intended to go north to the town of Manitou Springs. However, there are several "social" trails that criss-cross it and it is hard to follow. Notice the warning under "Hazards." If you hike it on foot, you will sec what I mean. We took the trail junctions toward the water-fall and kept choosing to go up and back to the Red Rocks Trail. We found ourselves on a very dangerous trail with no place to turn around. The trail was so narrow with loose foot-ing that we even had one horse loose her footing and fall to her side! Fortunately, no one was hurt, However, stay away from this!

Following the Red Rocks Trail up to the top is beautiful but not an easy ride. Much of the trail is narrow and the switch-back section has loose rock. When you get to the top, you will see the Crystal Park Trail going off to the west. Do not take this trail as it leads to a private housing development. As you stay on the trail you will go down through Bear Creek Canyon Park on the Palmer Trail. You will ride this all the way down to High Drive. You will then go with the traffic back to the parking area.

This is not an easy trail and should be avoided in the winter due to ice flows. Shoes would be recommended. The trail is too narrow to even considered ponying a second horse. However, the scenery is beautiful so if you want to tackle this one, do not take beginner horses or riders and make sure your horse is in good condition.

Mt. Herman - Monument Preserve - El Paso County

Travel Distance: 36.7 miles
Travel Time: 47 minutes
Travel Directions: Go south on I-25 for 35.4 miles. Take exit #161 at Monument. The exit curves back around facing north. At the light at the end of the exit turn left (west) onto Second Street. Turn left onto Mitchell Ave for 0.6 miles. Turn right onto Mt. Herman Road for 0.7 miles. Turn left at Schilling Avenue and take an immediate right into the Mt. Herman trailhead entrance.

Trailer Parking: Gravel pull-through parking lot that is big enough for 4 trailers. There is a second parking lot 0.6 miles farther down this road which is the base for the Monument Trail that goes up the valley on the south side of Mt. Herman. However, this is a very small lot, too small for trailers.
Fees: None

 100

Water: No
Restrooms: No
Length of Ride: 4.5 miles
Hazards: Hikers, bikers, dogs on leashes, wildlife.

Description of our ride: We had a lovely ride around the Monument Preserve area, a 1,000 acre open space. There are trails criss-crossing the entire area. We selected trails that took us in a northwesterly direction toward Monument Rock. This landmark made it easy to find our way around. After circling the rock, we rode south around the forest service property and back to the rock. Here we dismounted and had our lunch. We picked some trails that went east and south from the rock and then back to the parking lot. We rode for two hours but there were a lot of other trails that could be

Photo by Carol Crisp

explored. It was all an easy ride. The surface of the trail was usually just natural dirt. This would be a good beginner trail for horse and rider.

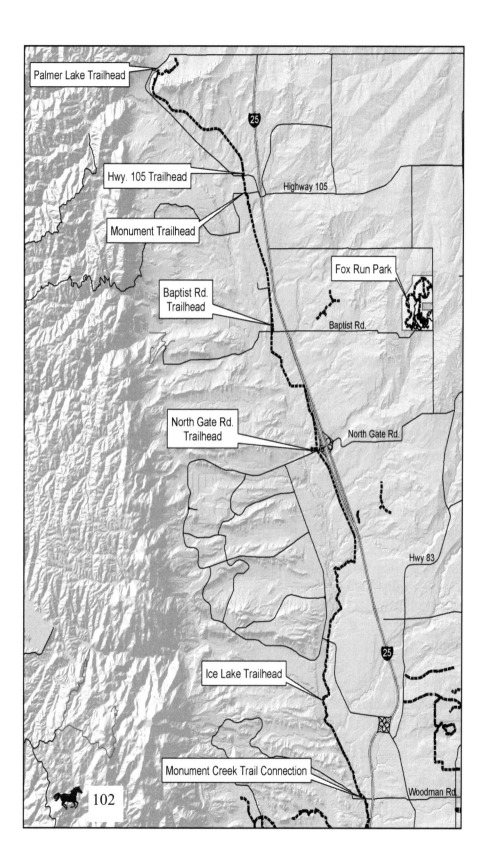

Palmer Lake Trailhead

Hwy. 105 Trailhead

Monument Trailhead

Baptist Rd.
Trailhead

North Gate Rd.
Trailhead

Ice Lake Trailhead

Monument Creek Trail Connection

Fox Run Park

Highway 105

Baptist Rd.

North Gate Rd.

Hwy 83

Woodman Rd.

102

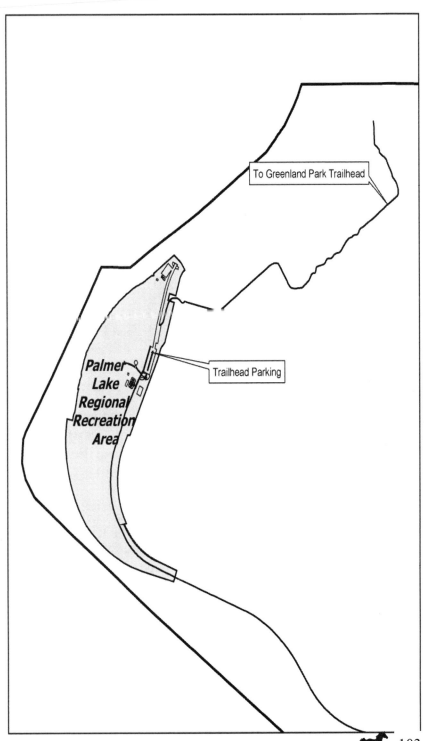

To Greenland Park Trailhead

Palmer Lake Regional Recreation Area

Trailhead Parking

103

New Santa Fe Trail - El Paso County

Travel Distance: 33.5 miles
Travel Time: 38 minutes
Travel Directions: Go south on I-25 for 33 miles to exit 161, the Monument Exit. At the end of the exit, go left (west) for 0.4 miles to Jefferson. Turn right onto Jefferson and drive 0.1 mile to 3rd street. Turn right onto 3rd. The trailhead is 1/2 block up on your right.

Trailer Parking: There is a gravel, turn-around parking lot. There is room for 3 or 4 trailers on the east side. The parking lot at the Baptist Road Exit is about the same.
Fees: None
Water: Drinking fountain is turned off in the winter.
Restrooms: Yes, Monument trailhead was locked for the winter. Baptist Road and Palmer Lake trailheads were open.
Length of Ride: From Monument north to Palmer Lake is 3.5 miles. From Monument south to Baptist Road is 2.5 miles.
Hazards: Walkers/joggers, dogs on leashes, bikers, street

crossings, sections of the north bound trail go near a railroad track. Both times we were there, a train came by at around 1:30. If you ride south, you will be going beside a rather busy street .

Description of our ride: The New Santa Fe Trail actually goes all the way down to Colorado Springs and connects to the city's Monument Creek Trail. Going north to Palmer Lake, it connects to the new Douglas County Greenland Open Space Trail. Therefore, you can ride for miles and miles on this easy, flat trail with great footing. We parked at both the Monument Trailhead and the Baptist Road Trailhead and rode north to Palmer Lake. The ride from Monument is much prettier and takes you through beautiful areas. However, sections of this part of the trail do go near a railroad track. Fortunately, the train came by after we were back at the parking lot. We started our ride from Monument by crossing a street at a protected crosswalk. We rode past a huge flock of Canadian Geese and past some houses that were being built. However, we were soon in open, undeveloped land and had a beautiful ride with great views of Mt. Herman. We did lots of trotting and cantering on this wonderful trail. We stopped for lunch at Palmer Lake then rode back. We did all of this in two hours. This is a great trail for conditioning and ponying another horse. Shoes would not be necessary.

Palmer Park- El Paso County

Travel Distance: 51.6 miles
Travel Time: 1 hour
Travel Directions: From I-25 and Lincoln, drive south on I-25 for 48.6 miles to exit #145, the Fillmore exit. Drive east on Fillmore for 2.5 miles. Turn left on Paseo by the Colorado Springs County Club. (Look for Union Street as it is the next street after Union.) Drive north for 0.5 miles. This street will take you straight into Palmer Park. Turn into the dirt area in front of the stables.

Trailer Parking: The only trailer parking is on the dirt area in front of the Mark Regner Stable so when you park, be courteous and do not block his trailers or access road. There is room for 5-6 trailers.
Fees: None
Water: Yes, there is a drinking fountain just to the east by the restrooms.

Restrooms: Yes, just to the east, however they are locked in the winter and a port-a-potty is brought in.

Length of Ride: We rode for 3 hours and covered 5.5 miles. That included a stop for lunch and lots of picture taking.

Hazards: Hikers, bikers, dogs on leashes (or *off* in our experience!), wildlife, road crossings within the park, wooden bridge over stream, for a short distance the Palmer Point Trail goes parallel to Austin Bluffs Parkway which is a very busy street. This trail also goes close to some backyards on the west side. At one point, the trail went between the legs of a high-power-line pole, some rocky areas. The highest bluff in the north area is called Yucca Flats and is an off-leash dog run area.

Description of our ride: We took the Palmer Point Trail to the west out of the parking lot and followed it to the north side of the park. We went past some homes, along Austin Bluffs Parkway and then got back into the trees. With the exception of that brief time, you feel like you are in the mountains and way away from civilization. This is such a beautiful, unspoiled park and such a gem right in the middle of Colorado Springs! We continued to follow the Palmer Point Trail. When we came to a gravel parking lot for a reservation only area, we found the Palmer Point trail on the opposite corner. After coming out of the trees, we noticed the Templeton Trail going off to the right. We took the second entrance and found that it is a lovely loop returning to the Palmer Point Trail. There are a couple of steep rock ridges to step up or down but not too difficult. We followed this trail until it ran beside a dirt park road. Across the road we found a picnic table and stopped for lunch. The Palmer Point Trail continued straight from the other side of the road where we crossed but we also found that it went off to the east from the picnic table. We rode to the east and wove through a beautiful wooded section until it started to double back. At this point we crossed the paved road and followed the signs pointing left to the Grandview and Cheyenne Trails. You must take this trail! The view at the top of the point truly is "Grand!" We had to stop for pictures for quite a while! We then followed the trail down from the viewpoint, going in a southerly direction until we found a sign pointing west for the Cheyenne Trail. This trail will take you back down through the canyon and back to the parking lot but we weren't quite ready to quit (are we ever?) so we took the right-hand junctions in the trail that took us back up to the Grandview Trail and went past the viewpoint again. When we got back to the point where we had joined up with this trail, by the road, we stayed straight on the Grandview Trail and followed it down the canyon and back to the parking lot.

Most of the trails are natural and narrow and in several places they are rocky. However, the rocks are rounded rather than sharp so our unshod horses didn't have a problem.

This is an incredible park and definitely a "four horse shoes up!" trail. It can be ridden any time of the year, however, some of the trails in the canyons might be icy in the winter. There are so many trails in this park that you could take several different routes. This park deserves more than just one visit!

Palmer Park is one of the parks that city founder, General William Jackson Palmer donated to the city. All in all, this far- sighted city planner, donated more that 2,000 acres of land to be preserved as park space.

St. Mary's Falls Trail- North Cheyenne Canyon Park-El Paso County

Travel Distance: 60 miles

Travel Time: 1 hour 15 minutes

Travel Directions: Go south on I-25 for 52.5 miles to Hwy. 24 (exit # 141 - Cimarron St.) Go west on Hwy. 24 for 1.5 miles. Turn left on 21st Street and drive 0.8 miles to Lower Gold Camp Road. Turn right on Lower Gold Camp Road and drive for 1.1 miles to Bear Creek Road (26th Street.) Turn left. Travel for 0.9 miles on this windy road. At the stop sign, take a sharp left turn onto Gold Camp Road. After 2.2 miles, this becomes a very narrow dirt road with sharp, blind turns. Fortunately, there is not much traffic but go slowly. Follow Gold Camp Road for a total of 3.9 miles to the parking lot above the Helen Hunt Falls. This will take you through two single lane tunnels so go slowly. Another option is to stop at the trailhead at the 2.9 mile point and ride the last mile through the tunnels. On weekdays there is not a lot of traffic on the road. I would recommend this option if you have a very long trailer.

Trailer Parking: An open gravel area is available with plenty of room for many trailers.

Fees: None

Water: Not at trailhead but you can find spots along Buffalo Creek.

Restroom: No

Length of Ride: 5.6 miles, 1.2 miles along Gold Camp Road Trail and 1.6 miles along St. Mary's Falls Trail and back.

Hazards: Caution: This trail is a dead-end at the falls. We took the trail to the base of the falls. We discovered that it is very narrow, and goes along a steep mountainside. The footing is loose as well. It is a dead end and it was difficult to turn our horses around. For this reason, I would stop in the trees about 50 feet back from the falls and hike in to see the falls. The trail is also used by hikers, wildlife, and mountain bikers. Gold Camp Road is a multi-use trail so motorcycles are allowed.

Description of our ride: The first 1.2 miles of this trail are along an old railroad bed. In the 1890's, a railroad carried gold ore from the mines in Cripple Creek to the smelter in Colorado Springs. It has now become a wonderful multi-use trail. From the parking lot, you will ride up this wide sand and dirt road. When you come to tunnel #3, which partially collapsed in 1988, you will take a narrow dirt trail around and over it. After coming down on the other side of the tunnel, you will stay to the right and follow along Buffalo Creek. The first mile of the trail along the creek is very easy and beautiful and only makes a gentle climb. It is single file and packed dirt with a few rocks. The last 0.6 miles leave the creek and start to climb steeply. The entire trail climbs 1,200 feet and most of the climb is in this last part. Within a short distance of the falls, you will decide if you want to go to the base of the falls or to the top. There is a metal sign that says "Base of Falls 500 feet" and points left. Below that it points right and says "Top of Falls 0.2 miles." We chose to go to the base. You will continue to climb and go through a narrow path...watch your knees on the trees and the rocks! As I said under the listing of hazards, the last 30 yards before the falls are dangerous. The trail is very narrow and goes along the steep sides of the mountain. The ground is soft and slides down the mountainside as you ride along. Added to this, the trail ends at the falls and there is very little room to turn around. So, stop at the last bend in the trail, just as it comes out of the trees. Walk up to see the falls. The falls are more accurately described as a 40 foot long waterslide. It is very beautiful and you will also enjoy the view of the pine and blue spruce drainage that goes down the mountain clear to the Broadmore Hotel.

We did not go to the top of the falls. At this time, the trails beyond the falls at the top are in bad shape and not clearly marked so I would recommend turning back at the falls.

Most of the trail is packed dirt. There were only a few rocky places. Therefore, you could get by without shoes.

Stratton Open Space

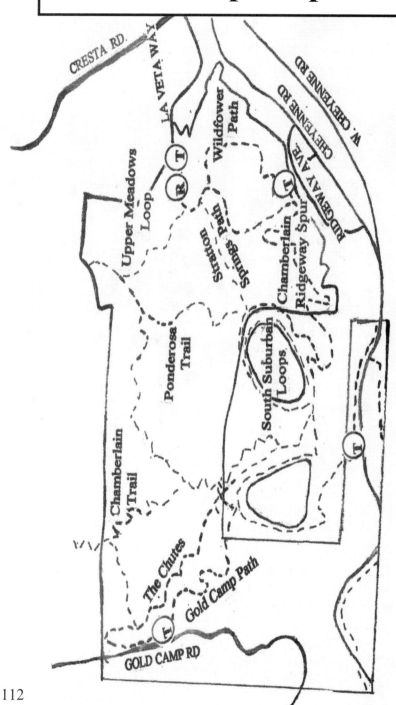

Stratton Open Space at Cheyenne Canon Park-El Paso County

Travel Distance: 57 miles
Travel Time: 1 hour 10 minutes
Travel Directions: Go south on I-25 for 52.5 miles to Hwy. 24 (exit # 141 - Cimarron St.) Go west on Hwy. 24 for 1.5 miles. Turn left on 21st Street and drive for 3.0 miles to Cheyenne Blvd. Turn right and drive for 0.4 miles to Ridgeway Ave. Watch carefully for the brown sign. Go right for 0.1 miles. The trailhead is on your right.

Trailer Parking: This is a paved parking lot with two designated horse trailer spots.
Fees: None
Water: No, but there is a drinking fountain at the LaVetta Way trailhead.
Restroom: Not at this trailhead but you can ride over to the LaVetta Way trailhead where they have nice restrooms.

Length of Ride: We covered 6.5 miles in 2.5 hours including a lunch stop.

Hazards: Hikers, bikers, dogs on leashes, some low branches and narrow trails through trees. The most dangerous part was on the Chamberlain Ridgeway Spur that goes around Gold Camp Reservoir. The reservoir has a barbwire-topped fence that leans out toward you and was right at my eye level.

Description of our ride: This City of Colorado Springs park is 318 acres in size and boasts 5 ecosystems. We started our ride by going on the Chamberlain Ridgeway Spur which is 1 mile long and ends at a parking lot along North Cheyenne Road. This trail takes you up to the Twin Mesa Reservoir and around the Gold Camp Reservoir. We didn't like being so close to the barbwire fence that surrounds the reservoir. We then rode back and found ourselves wandering around trails. At times we were on the Ponderosa Trail, at times we were on the Chutes Trail and at times we were on the Chamberlain Trail. We eventually ended up on the Upper Meadows Loop and followed it back to the trailhead. The Chutes Trail is a 1.02 mile trail that climbs up to Gold Camp Road. It is a favorite trail for mountain bikers as they love to come zooming down the "chute." So, beware on crowded weekends! We found this park to be a work in progress with lots of unmarked trails going off in different directions . Anything marked a "path" is hiker only. All others are open for equestrians. You can spend most of the day riding around the trails as they wind from meadow to wood. We covered 6.5 miles of trails in 2 hours and didn't cover everything.

This open space area was named for millionaire miner and philanthropist Winfield Scott Stratton and is the result of the donations of many organizations. Most of the trails are packed dirt with some loose rock areas. Shoes are not required.

RIDING COLORADO

JEFFERSON COUNTY

Maps courtesy of Jefferson County Parks and Open Space

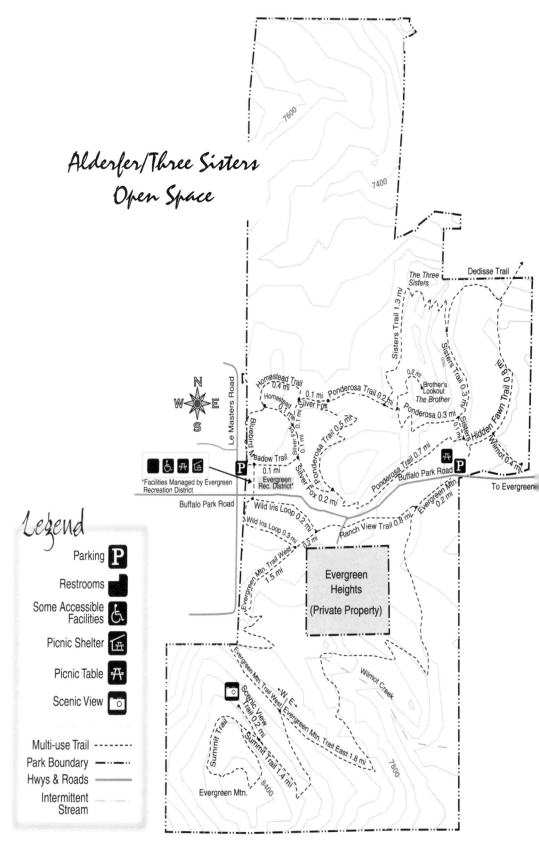

Alderfer/Three Sisters Open Space

7600

7400

The Three Sisters

Dedisse Trail

Sisters Trail 1.3 mi

Sisters Trail 0.3 mi

Brother's Lookout
The Brother

0.2 mi

Homestead Trail 0.4 mi

Homestead 0.1 mi

Ponderosa Trail 0.2 mi

Silver Fox

Ponderosa 0.3 mi

Silver Fox 0.1 mi

Ponderosa Trail 0.5 mi

Ponderosa Trail 0.7 mi

Hidden Fawn Trail 0.8 mi

Wilmot 0.4 mi

Le Masters Road

Bluebird Meadow Trail

Silver Fox 0.2 mi

0.1 mi
Evergreen Rec. District*

*Facilities Managed by Evergreen Recreation District

Buffalo Park Road

Wild Iris Loop 0.2 mi

Wild Iris Loop 0.3 mi

Ranch View Trail 0.8 mi

Buffalo Park Road

Evergreen Mtn. 0.2 mi

To Evergreen

Evergreen Mtn. Trail West 1.5 mi

Evergreen Heights

(Private Property)

Wilmot Creek

7800

Evergreen Mtn. Trail West / Evergreen Mtn. Trail East 1.8 mi

Scenic View Trail 0.2 mi

Summit Trail 1.4 mi

Summit Trail

8400

Evergreen Mtn.

Legend

Parking	**P**
Restrooms	
Some Accessible Facilities	
Picnic Shelter	
Picnic Table	
Scenic View	

Multi-use Trail — — — —
Park Boundary — · — · —
Hwys & Roads ————
Intermittent Stream

Alderfer Three Sisters Open Space - Jefferson County

Photo by Carol Crisp

Travel Distance: 46 miles
Travel Time: 55 minutes
Travel Directions: From Lincoln, go north on I-25 for 0.9 miles to the C-470 exit going west. Go west on C-470 for 27.6 miles to the I-70 west exit. Go west on I-70 for 8.3 miles to the Evergreen exit #252. Go straight through the light toward Bergen Park and downtown Evergreen for 7.3 miles. Turn right onto Hwy.73 for 0.6 miles. Turn right at the light onto Buffalo Park Road and go for 1.5 miles to the La Masters Road park entrance.

Trailer Parking: Designated trailer parking is on the left side of the parking lot as you enter. There is room for 3 or 4 trailers. It is a gravel parking lot with easy turn around.
Fees: None

Water: No

Restrooms: Yes, outhouse

Length of Ride: We rode for 3 hours and covered over 5 miles.

Hazards: You must cross Buffalo Park Road to get to the south side of the park. You will share the trail with dogs on leashes, mountain bikers, hikers and wildlife.

Description of our ride: Alderfer Three Sisters Open Space is a beautiful park of 1,100 acres with a variety of scenery from open meadows to thick ponderosa pine forests. There are four rock formations in the north part of the park called the Three Sisters and a Brother. There are 12.5 miles of trails for riding.

We began our ride by crossing Buffalo Park Road and riding in the south side of the park. We followed Evergreen Mountain Trail west as it made a gradual climb past a beautiful granite outcropping. We turned right onto the Summit Trail and rode 1.4 miles up to the top for a beautiful view of the Continental Divide. This was a "must see!" We rode back down, taking a right onto Evergreen Mountain Trail east and took this trail all the way back to the east parking lot where we stopped for lunch.

After lunch, we explored several of the trails on the north side of the park. We followed the Ponderosa trail to Brother's Lookout. We continued on the Ponderosa Trail to the Homestead Trail then back to the parking lot on the Bluebird Meadow Trail. The two sides of the park were completely different and both worth exploring. This was a very peaceful park without a lot of hazards for your horse. The trails were packed dirt for the most part with some rocky areas. The unshod horses didn't have a problem.

A large portion of the park was a gift from E. J. Alderfer and the Spencer Wyant Families. The Alderfers purchased the property in 1945. On it they raised silver foxes, cattle and horses as well as running a sawmill and a haying operation.

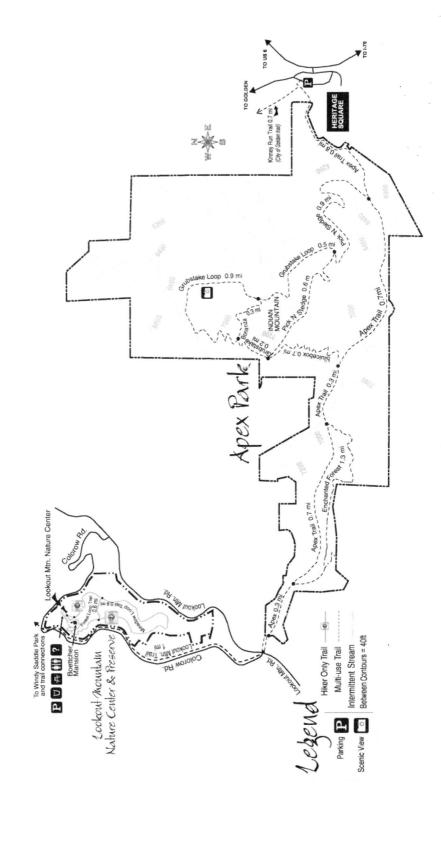

Apex Park - Jefferson County

Travel Distance: 30 miles
Travel Time: 35 minutes
Travel Directions: From Lincoln, go north on I-25 for 0.9 miles to the C-470 exit going west. Go west on C-470 for 27.6 miles to the I-70 west exit. Go west on I-70 for 1.2 miles to the first exit, exit #259. From this exit turn right (north) on Hwy. 40 for 1 mile. The entrance to Heritage Square is on your left.

Trailer Parking: Park in the lowest (eastern) parking lot. The trailhead is on the north end of the parking lot. This is a paved parking lot that you will share with people who are taking the shuttle up to Central City. There is a hitching post and a picnic table.
Fees: None
Water: No, horses can drink from the creek
Restrooms: Yes, outhouse
Length of Ride: We rode for 3 hours and covered

over 5 miles.

Hazards: This is a popular trail for mountain bikes but everyone that we ran into was very courteous about yielding the right of way. You will also come across hikers, dogs on leashes, bridges and a small water crossing on the Enchanted Forest Trail.

Description of our ride: I was so excited to find such a beautiful trail so close in. Apex Park is easy to get to, but once you are there you leave the rest of the world behind as the trail winds up the canyon and through the woods. We rode up the Apex Trail for 2.5 miles. It follows along beside a small stream. We were on the north side of the stream so we were in the sun and did not have any snow. However, when we turned left onto the west end of the Enchanted Forest Loop, we were riding in a lot of snow and some very icy parts. We eventually turned around before finishing this loop and went back to the Apex Trail the way we came. The Enchanted Forest Trail was a beautiful ride through dense forest. Obviously, the snow would not be a problem later in the spring. There are several other loops off of the Apex Trail going north up the mountain. The Apex Trail was very rocky at the beginning, getting less so as you travel up. It is a steady climb and I was glad I was on a horse instead of on one of those bikes! Our horses were not shod so we went slowly through the rocky parts. Shoes and conditioning would be recommended.

Apex Park has an interesting history. In the 1860's and 1870's, this canyon was the site of one of three wagon roads going up to the Central City (then known as Gregory Diggings) gold mines. This old road had been a toll road and you would have had to pay $0.10 per riding horse! In 1878-79 a flood wiped out most of the road and the owners could not afford to rebuild it.

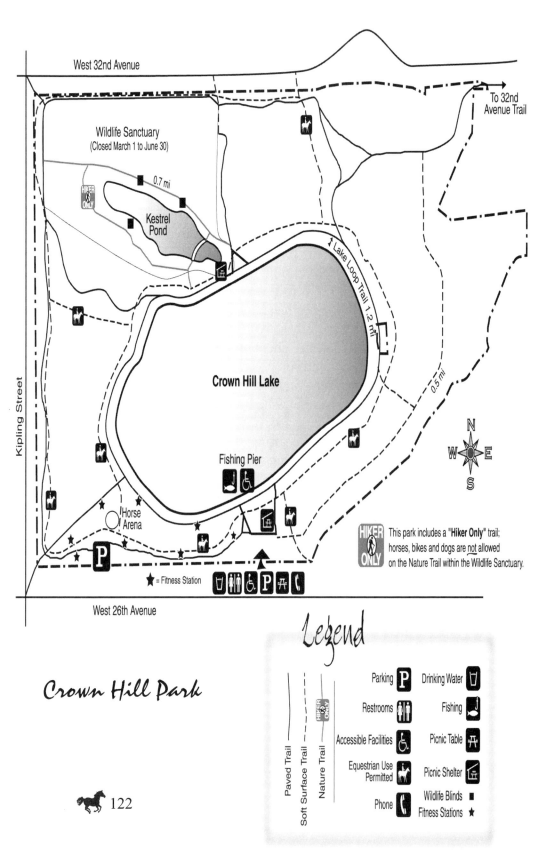

West 32nd Avenue

To 32nd Avenue Trail

Wildlife Sanctuary
(Closed March 1 to June 30)

0.7 mi

HIKER ONLY

Kestrel Pond

Lake Loop Trail 1.2 mi

Kipling Street

Crown Hill Lake

0.5 mi

N
W   E
S

Fishing Pier

Horse Arena

HIKER ONLY

This park includes a "**Hiker Only**" trail; horses, bikes and dogs are not allowed on the Nature Trail within the Wildlife Sanctuary.

★ = Fitness Station

West 26th Avenue

Crown Hill Park

122

Crown Hill Park - Jefferson County

Travel Distance: 22.7 miles
Travel Time: 37 minutes
Travel Directions: From Lincoln, go north on I-25 for 16.4 miles to the 6th Avenue West Exit. Go west on 6th Avenue for 5.2 miles to Kipling. Go north on Kipling for 2.0 miles to 26th. Turn right on 26th. The parking lot is on your left.

Trailer Parking: Designated trailer parking on the left side of the parking lot as you enter. There is room for 2 trailers. Paved surface. Picnic tables.
Fees: None
Water: At the other parking lot to the east.
Restrooms: Yes, at the other parking lot to the east.
Length of Ride: We rode for 45 minutes at a fairly fast pace.
Hazards: Urban park so lots of traffic if you take the exterior loop trails. Hikers, bikers, rollerbladers, dogs on leashes.

Description of our ride: This is a pleasant urban park that

123

has reserved some space for riders. Right by the parking lot is a small arena that is maintained by the City of Lakewood. After working my horse for 15 minutes in the arena we rode on the horse trail that goes on the west side of Crown Hill Lake. We followed this trail, taking the outer loops where possible and headed east along a narrow dirt trail all the way to the Crown Hill Cemetery boundaries. We looped back to the parking lot along the most southern trail. We kept up a trot most of the time and did the entire loop in 45 minutes including a few side trips to explore off-shoots. You could make the ride a bit longer if you took the most extreme western trail that goes along Kipling.

This is an easy trail. No shoes would be required and it is a good place to condition a horse.

This area was once a farm, boasting the first apple orchard in Wheat Ridge. In 1972, the West Aspen Company of Texas wanted to develop the land around the lake into a residential community for 8,000 people in high rise apartments. The citizens of the area worked together to enable the cities of Wheat Ridge and Lakewood and Jefferson County to acquire the 177 acre park and keep it in a fairly natural state.

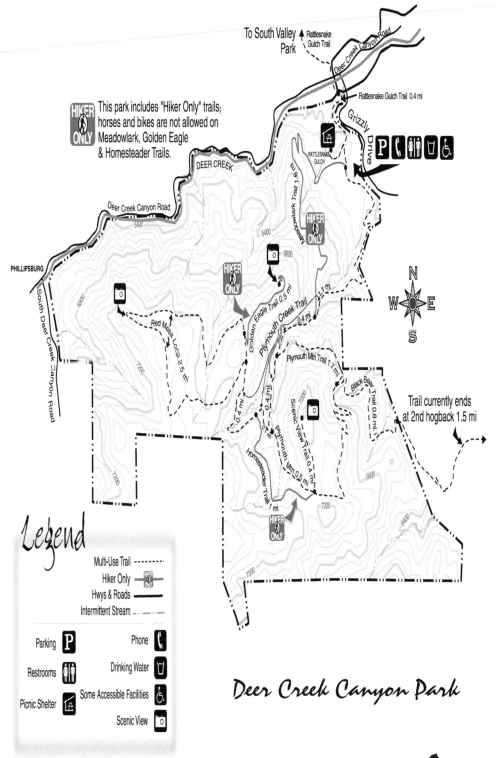

This park includes "Hiker Only" trails; horses and bikes are not allowed on Meadowlark, Golden Eagle & Homesteader Trails.

To South Valley Park

Rattlesnake Gulch Trail

Deer Creek Canyon Road

Rattlesnake Gulch Trail 0.4 mi

Grizzly Drive

RATTLESNAKE GULCH

DEER CREEK

Deer Creek Canyon Road

6400

6400

PHILLIPSBURG

6800

6800

South Deer Creek Canyon Road

6800

Red Mesa Loop 2.5 mi

Meadowlark Trail 1.9 mi

Golden Eagle Trail 0.5 mi

Plymouth Creek Trail

1.1 mi

0.4 mi

Plymouth Mtn Trail 1.7 mi

Black Bear Trail 0.8 mi

7200

7200

0.4 mi

0.4 mi

0.4 mi

Scenic View Trail 0.4 mi

7200

6800

Trail currently ends at 2nd hogback 1.5 mi

Homesteader Trail 1 mi

Plymouth Mtn 0.5 mi

7200

6400

7200

N W E S

Legend

Multi-Use Trail	-------
Hiker Only	
Hwys & Roads	———
Intermittent Stream	

Parking	**P**	Phone		
Restrooms		Drinking Water		
Picnic Shelter		Some Accessible Facilities		
		Scenic View		

Deer Creek Canyon Park

125

Deer Creek Canyon Park -
Jefferson County

Travel Distance: 17.3 miles
Travel Time: 30 minutes
Travel Directions: From Lincoln, go north on I-25 for 0.9 miles to the C-470 exit going west. Go west on C-470 for 12.2 miles to the Wadsworth Exit. At the stop light at the bottom of the exit turn left (south) onto Wadsworth and get into the right lane immediately. Take the first right which is 0.3 miles away onto Deer Creek Canyon Road. Turn right and drive for 1.5 miles to the stop sign. Turn left (watch out for the blind corner.) Go 2.0 miles to Grizzly Road and take a left. Proceed for 0.4 miles and turn right into the parking lot. Trailer parking is to the left.

Trailer Parking: Designated trailer parking on the left side of the parking lot as you enter. There is room for 5 or 6 trailers depending upon how tightly you pack in. Paved surface. Pic-

 126

nic tables are available at the trailhead.

Fees: None

Water: Yes

Restrooms: Yes, the nicest we've seen!

Length of Ride: We rode for 3 hours and covered over 7 miles

Hazards: The low part of the trail is very rocky with loose sharp rocks. There are a few small water crossings in the spring. Some of the trails are narrow with steep drop offs. The trail climbs steeply. You will share the trail with dogs on leashes, mountain bikers and hikers.

Description of our ride: From the parking lot, we followed the Plymouth Creek Trail. This is a steep, rocky trail but very pretty. In the spring there are lovely waterfalls. We turned left at the Plymouth Ridge Trail and continued our climb. The trail got better the higher up we went. We turned right onto the Scenic View Trail and stopped there for lunch. You have beautiful views to the east from this point. Most of us had to get back to meet school buses so we went back the way we came. However, Carol continued west and rode the Red Mesa Loop as well. That made it an eleven mile ride for her.

There are 7.5 miles of trails, a few of which are for hikers only. Going out and back or taking one of the loops gives you plenty of miles to cover for a lovely day ride. However, your horse needs to be in good condition as the climb is steep and I would recommend shoes, as the lower part is quite rocky.

Deer Creek Park was once a campground for wandering bands of Ute and Arapahoe Indians. Its most infamous resident was Alfred Packer, Colorado's famous cannibal. When he was paroled from the state penitentiary in 1901, he lived in a cabin in Phillipsburg and worked the mines and ranches in the Deer Creek area. This park is one of the few areas in Jefferson County that is home to Gamble Oak, making it a great place to go in the fall!

Elk Meadow Park

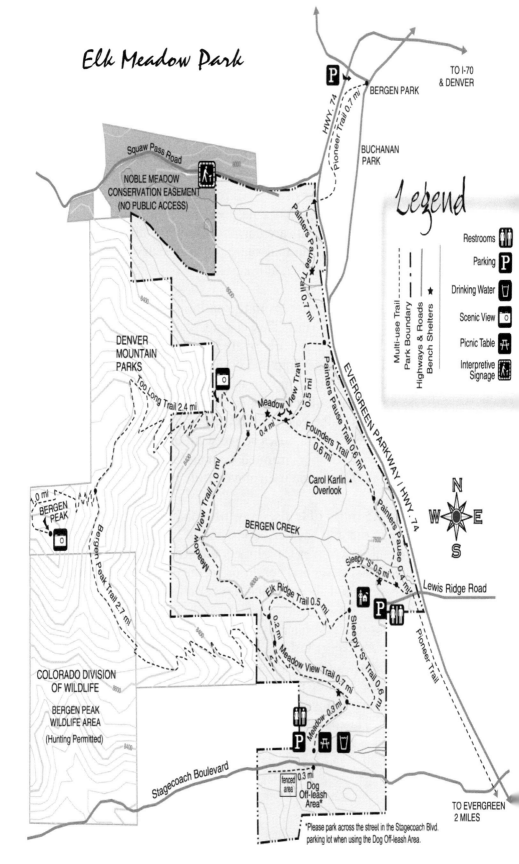

TO I-70 & DENVER

BERGEN PARK

BUCHANAN PARK

Pioneer Trail 0.7 mi

HWY. 74

Squaw Pass Road

NOBLE MEADOW CONSERVATION EASEMENT (NO PUBLIC ACCESS)

Painters Pause Trail 0.7 mi

Legend

Restrooms	
Parking	P
Drinking Water	
Scenic View	
Picnic Table	
Interpretive Signage	

Multi-use Trail
Park Boundary
Highways & Roads
★ Bench Shelters

DENVER MOUNTAIN PARKS

Too Long Trail 2.4 mi

Meadow View Trail 0.4 mi

Painters Pause Trail 0.5 mi

Founders Trail 0.6 mi

Painters Pause Trail 0.6 mi

Carol Karlin Overlook

EVERGREEN PARKWAY / HWY. 74

1.0 mi

BERGEN PEAK

Meadow View Trail 1.0 mi

BERGEN CREEK

7600

Painters Pause 0.4 mi

Bergen Peak Trail 2.7 mi

Sleepy "S" 0.5 mi

Lewis Ridge Road

Elk Ridge Trail 0.5 mi

0.2 mi

P

Sleepy "S" Trail 0.6 mi

Meadow View Trail 0.7 mi

Pioneer Trail

COLORADO DIVISION OF WILDLIFE

BERGEN PEAK WILDLIFE AREA

(Hunting Permitted)

Meadow 0.3 mi

P

fenced area

0.3 mi Dog Off-leash Area*

Stagecoach Boulevard

TO EVERGREEN 2 MILES

*Please park across the street in the Stagecoach Blvd. parking lot when using the Dog Off-leash Area.

N W E S

Elk Meadow - Jefferson County

Travel Distance: 40.1 miles
Travel Time: 45 minutes
Travel Directions: From Lincoln, go north on I-25 for 0.9 miles to the C-470 exit going west. Go west on C-470 for 27.6 miles to the I-70 west exit. Go west on I-70 for 8.3 miles to the Evergreen exit # 252. Go straight through the light at the end of the exit toward Bergen Park on Hwy. 74. Stay on this road for 5 miles. Take a sharp right onto Lewis Ridge Road and right into the trailhead. Horse trailer parking is only available at the Lewis Ridge Road parking area.

Trailer Parking: Designated trailer parking with room for 4 or 5 trailers is on the upper side of this parking lot. Gravel parking lot has straight in and out parking along the side. It was a crowded lot even on a weekday so expect even more on the weekends!
Fees: None

Water: Not at this trail head but there is water at the parking lot off Stagecoach Blvd. You can ride over to it but that won't do your horse a lot of good on a hot day.

Restrooms: Yes, port-a-potty

Length of Ride: We rode for 3 hours and covered 4.7 miles. There are 12 miles of trails so you can pick several routes.

Hazards: Hikers, dogs on leashes, bikers.

Description of our ride: Jefferson County has been blessed with beautiful land and has blessed the rest of us by making a lot of this land public parks! Elk Meadow Park is a huge park with 12 miles of trails going through a variety of terrain. We started our ride by heading up the mountainside on the Sleepy S Trail. We took a left onto the Meadow Trail to see the other parking area. That area has water and nice restrooms but no trailer parking! We then backtracked to the trail junction and turned left onto the Meadow View Trail. The Bergen Peak Trail goes off of this trail if you want a much longer and steeper ride. It would be worth it if your horse is in condition! We followed the Meadow View Trail for nearly 2 miles, stopping for lunch at a pretty vista along the way. The trail skirts along the side of the mountain ridge through a beautiful forest then cuts back down to the meadow. While in the forest, look for the Tassel Eared Albert's squirrel. At the meadow we turned right onto Founders Trail and rode through the meadow to Painters Pause Trail which took us back to the parking area.

This trail is packed dirt in the mountains and sand in the meadow. Shoes would not be necessary for the route we took but if you want to climb to Bergen Peak I would recommend them.

The charming barn in the meadow is evidence of the ranching history of this property, once home to several ranchers who ran herds of cattle on the property. Jefferson County began purchasing this property in 1977.

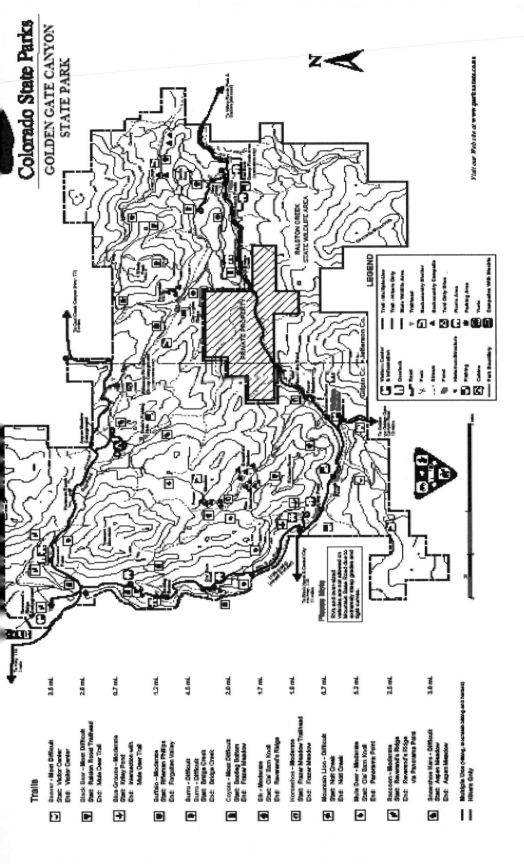

Colorado State Parks

GOLDEN GATE CANYON STATE PARK

Visit our Web site at www.parks.state.co.us

Golden Gate Canyon State Park - Jefferson County

Travel Distance: 51 miles

Travel Time: 1 hour and 20 minutes

Travel Directions: From Lincoln, go north on I-25 for 0.9 miles to the C-470 exit going west. Go west on C-470 for 26.2 miles to the I-70 junction. Stay to the left toward Grand Junction but do not get onto I-70. Continue straight toward Golden on Highway 6. Proceed west for 4.5 miles to the signal. Go through the light onto Hwy. 93 for 1.4 miles to Golden Gate Canyon Drive. Turn left. Drive 13 miles to the Golden Gate Canyon Park entrance. You may either turn to the right at the visitor's center and park at the Nott Creek Trailhead or continue on the same road to the Kriley Pond Trailhead. You could also drive clear around the north side of the park to the Aspen Meadow Campground which has trailer parking and Equestrian Camp sites.

Trailer Parking: Circular paved road that will hold 3 or 4 small trailers.

Fees: $5

Water: Not at Kriley Pond Trailhead.

Restrooms: Yes, outhouse

Length of Ride: We rode for 3 hours including a stop at Panorama Point for lunch and to enjoy the view.

Hazards: The Mule Deer Trail is extremely steep and rocky and one that I will not ride again with my dressage horse as it is too risky! A few small water crossings. Hikers, dogs on leashes, bikers, wildlife.

Description of our ride: We followed the Blue Grouse Trail for 0.7 miles then turned right onto the Mule Deer Trail. This is a beautiful trail for several miles as it passes through Aspen Groves and Pine Trees. It takes you past the backcountry campsites at Frazer Meadow. However, as you get near Gap Road, you will climb up the north side of Tremont Mountain on a very steep and rocky trail that was difficult for the horses to navigate. Once we got over that, we rode to Panorama Point and stopped for lunch. The Mule Deer Trail is 5.2 miles from Ole' Barn Knoll to Panorama Point. This is a beautiful place with views to die for! From this point, you can see more than 100 miles of the peaks along the Continental Divide! After lunch and getting our fill of the scenery, we looped down hill on the Raccoon trail which will connect you to the Elk Trail after 2 miles. We followed the Elk Trail for 1.7 miles to the Ole' Barn Knoll where we picked up the Mule Deer Trail again and followed it back to the Blue Grouse Cut Off and back to the parking lot. If I were to ride this again, I would go left at the end of Blue Grouse trail, follow it up to Panorama Point, take the loop on Raccoon and back down Elk to Mule Deer to Blue Grouse to the trailhead. That would be a beautiful ride without the dangerous parts.

Golden Gate Canyon Park covers 14,000 gorgeous acres! It's elevation ranges from 7,600 to 10,400 feet. You can see the land as it was seen 100 years ago by Indians, trappers, gold miners, and lumberjacks.

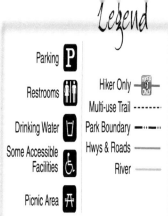

Legend

Parking	**P**	Hiker Only	▦
Restrooms	🚻	Multi-use Trail	- - - -
Drinking Water	🚰	Park Boundary	-·-·-·
Some Accessible Facilities	♿	Hwys & Roads	———
Picnic Area	🅰	River	———

Lair O' the Bear Park

HIKER ONLY This park includes "Hiker Only" trails. Horses, bikes and dogs are not allowed on Creekside Loop. Also, horses and bikes are not allowed in the Creekside Trail/picnic area.

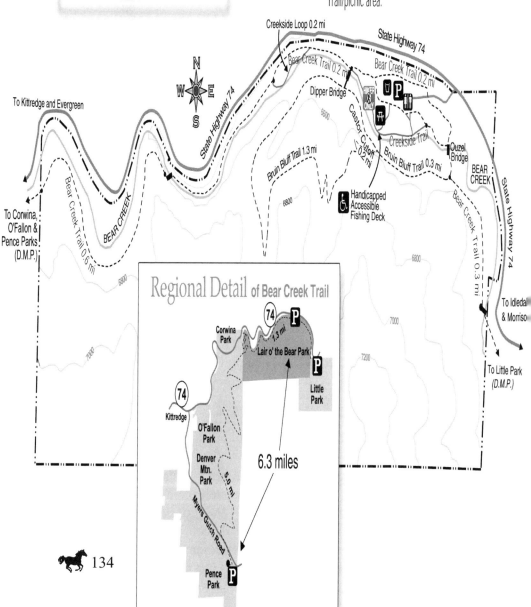

Creekside Loop 0.2 mi

State Highway 74

Bear Creek Trail 0.2 mi

Bear Creek Trail 0.2 mi

To Kittredge and Evergreen

State Highway 74

Dipper Bridge

Castor Cutoff 0.2 mi

Creekside Trail

Ouzel Bridge

6800

Bruin Bluff Trail 1.3 mi

Bruin Bluff Trail 0.3 mi

BEAR CREEK

State Highway 74

To Corwina, O'Fallon & Pence Parks (D.M.P.)

Bear Creek Trail 0.6 mi

BEAR CREEK

6800

Handicapped Accessible Fishing Deck

Bear Creek Trail 0.3 mi

6800

To Idleda & Morriso

To Little Park (D.M.P.)

Regional Detail of Bear Creek Trail

74

Corwina Park

1.3 mi

Lair o' the Bear Park

74

Kittredge

O'Fallon Park

Denver Mtn. Park

5.0 mi

Little Park

7000

7200

6.3 miles

Myers Gulch Road

🐎 134

Pence Park

Lair O' the Bear - Jefferson County

Travel Distance: 36.4 miles
Travel Time: 36 minutes
Travel Directions: From Lincoln, go north on I-25 for 0.9 miles to the C-470 exit going west. Go west on C-470 for 22.2 miles to the Morrison Road (Hwy. 8) exit. Go west on Hwy. 8, which becomes Hwy. 74, for 5.2 miles. Turn left into the park.

Trailer Parking: Large designated trailer parking, room for several trailers. Gravel parking lot with easy turn around. Picnic tables and barbecues.
Fees: None
Water: Yes, but shut off during the winter.
Restrooms: Yes
Length of Ride: We rode for 3 hours and covered 5 miles. There are 2.5 miles of trails that we rode in each direction.
Hazards: Bridges and water crossings. Narrow trees to ride between. Some slick rocks. Hikers, dogs on

leashes, bikers.

Description of our ride:
We rode west along the river for 1.2 miles until we came to the western boundary of the park. At this point, the trail goes left into O'Fallon Park. This trail goes through dense forest that opens out for beautiful vistas near the top. We rode for 1.5 miles to the top and over the ridge. This is a 6.3 mile long trail that connects O'Fallon Park, Denver Mountain Park and Pence Park. It is called the Bear Creek Trail. (See detail on map.) Two of our riders continued on for the remaining 4 miles to Pence Park. They reported that it wasn't necessary to go all the way to the end because all you find is a parking lot on the south side of Meyers Gulch Road. There is a beautiful meadow before you cross the road that would be a great place to have a picnic and then turn back there. The rest of us needed to meet school buses so we turned around and rode back over the ridge and down the hill. This is a beautiful park but your horse needs to be in good condition for the climb. The unshod horses did fine.

Just a note: Don't try to cross Hwy. 74 to get to Corwina Park. The road is much too busy and full of blind corners so drivers can't see you crossing.

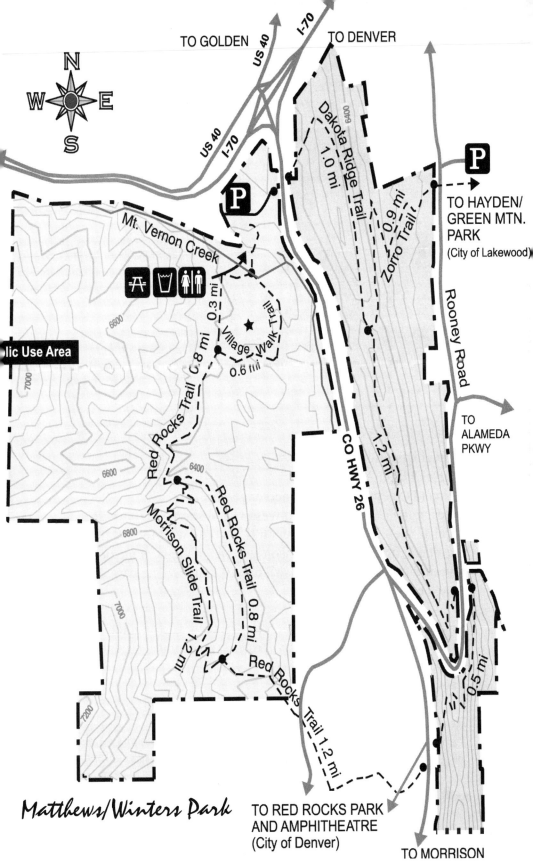

Matthews/Winters Park

Matthews/Winters Park, Dakota Ridge Trail-Jefferson County

Travel Distance: 28.3 miles

Travel Time: 31 minutes

Travel Directions: From Lincoln, go north on I-25 for 0.9 miles to the C-470 exit going west. Go west on C-470 for 26.2 miles to the I-70 junction. Get on I-70 going west for 1 mile to the first exit, #259, the Morrison Exit. At the light at the bottom of the exit, turn left and drive for 0.2 miles. The park entrance is on your right.

Trailer parking: Space enough for 3 trailers is straight ahead along the right side of the gravel road. You can turn around at the barn up ahead.

Fees: None

Water: No but horses could use the creek by the parking lot.

Restrooms: Yes

Length of Ride: We rode for 3.5 hours, counting a 1/2 hour stop for lunch at a cautious pace and covered 6.5 miles. We

 138

combined the Red Rocks Trail with the Dakota Ridge Trail.

Hazards: The Dakota Ridge Trail is a treacherous trail for expert riders and sure-footed, dependable horses, and for both riders and horses that are not afraid of heights! In places, this trail, which runs right across the top of the hogback called Dinosaur Ridge, is very narrow with steep cliffs dropping off on both sides! It is very rocky with uneven footing and slick rock surfaces. It is definitely an adrenaline rush but not for the faint of heart. When I say the views are breathtaking, I mean, in this case, you might be holding your breath the whole way! Just when you think you have it conquered and you're on your way down, up it goes again. It reminded me of the sign on I-70 that tells truckers not to be fooled, they aren't down yet! After getting down, we all decided we deserved T-shirts that read: "I survived the Dakota Ridge Trail!" You will have to cross Highway 26 to get there and to get back, and you have to ride a little way along the Dinosaur Ridge Road near the south end. This is also a favorite trail for mountain bikers. To make this a loop you will have to ride along the shoulder of a road for a short distance to get to the south end of the Red Rocks Trail.

Description of our ride: I think the hazard section adequately describes our ride!

Matthews/Winters Park, Red Rocks Trail-Jefferson County

Travel Distance: 28.3 miles

Travel Time: 31 minutes

Travel Directions: From Lincoln, go north on I-25 for 0.9 miles to the C-470 exit going west. Go west on C-470 for 26.2 miles to the I-70 junction. Get on I-70 going west for 1 mile to the first exit, #259, the Morrison Exit. At the light at the bottom of the exit, turn left and drive for 0.2 miles. The park entrance is on your right.

Trailer parking: Space enough for 3 trailers is straight ahead along the right side of the gravel road. You can turn around at the barn up ahead.

Fees: None

Water: No, but the horses could drink from the creek.

Restrooms: Yes

Length of Ride: We rode for 3.5 hours, counting a 1/2 hour stop for lunch, at a cautious pace and covered 6.5 miles. We

 140

combined the Red Rocks Trail with the Dakota Ridge Trail. Please read the information on the Dakota Ridge Trail before you ride it.

Hazards: A few small water crossings. Hikers, dogs on leashes, bikers. If you follow the Red Rocks Trail to get to the Dakota Ridge Trail, you will have to ride along a road for a short way, across a bridge and cross Hwy. 26. Hwy. 26 is not too busy during the middle of the weekday but can get busy on the weekends.

Description of our ride: Matthews/Winters Park is a fabulously beautiful park with its red rock formations and green juniper. We had the added advantage of riding it in May when the wild roses and other wild flowers were abundant. There are so many beautiful vistas that we had to keep stopping to take pictures. We started our ride by crossing Mt. Vernon Creek and riding up the Red Rocks Trail past a cemetery that still has a few gravestones probably from residents of the town of Mt. Vernon. The Village Walk Trail is an interesting walking tour of the old town of Mt. Vernon. At the trail junction we took the right side onto the Morrison Slide Trail. At the top, we stopped to have lunch. Parts of this trail are rocky or go over sheets of red rock. The switch backs are quite sharp. However, the views are worth it! When this trail meets up again with the Red Rocks Trail, you can take a left and do a nice loop back to the parking lot. This makes a lovely ride. However, we chose to go to the right and cross Highway 26 to get to the south end of the Dakota Ridge Trail. Do not ride this route without reading the Dakota Ridge write-up!

Matthews/Winters Park is a result of a series of purchases and donations for Jefferson County Open Space beginning in 1976. The park includes the site of the old town of Mt. Vernon, founded in 1859 as a gate keeper to the road up to the gold fields in Central City. This trail is good for the intermediate rider. It is a bit rocky but our shoeless horses did fine.

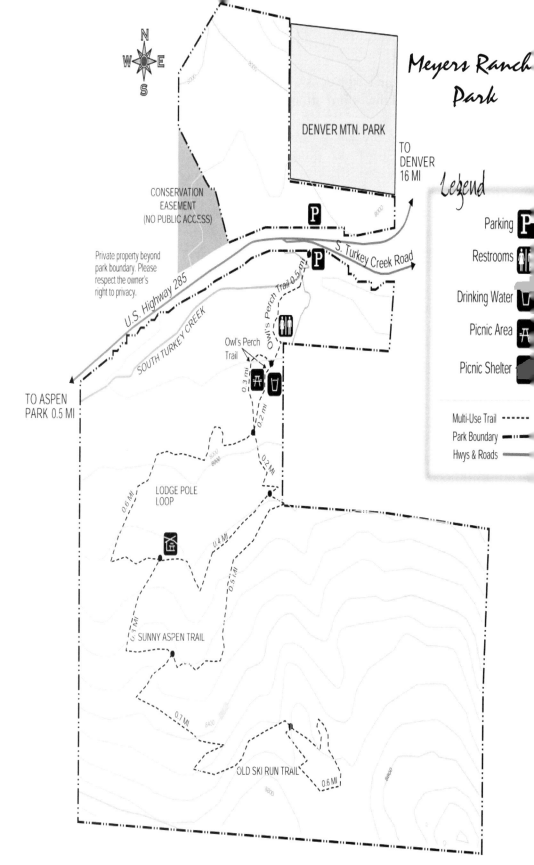

Meyers Ranch Park

DENVER MTN. PARK

TO DENVER 16 MI

CONSERVATION EASEMENT (NO PUBLIC ACCESS)

Private property beyond park boundary. Please respect the owner's right to privacy.

U.S. Highway 285

S. Turkey Creek Road

SOUTH TURKEY CREEK

TO ASPEN PARK 0.5 MI

Owl's Perch Trail 0.5 mi

Owl's Perch Trail

0.3 mi

0.2 mi

0.2 MI

LODGE POLE LOOP

0.6 MI

0.4 MI

0.5 MI

0.3 MI

SUNNY ASPEN TRAIL

0.7 MI

OLD SKI RUN TRAIL

0.6 MI

Legend

Parking	P
Restrooms	
Drinking Water	
Picnic Area	A
Picnic Shelter	

Multi-Use Trail - - - - -
Park Boundary ▪-▪-▪
Hwys & Roads ═══

Meyers Ranch Park-
Jefferson County

Travel Distance: 31 miles
Travel Time: 40 minutes
Travel Directions: Go North on I-25 for 0.9 miles. Exit onto C-470 going west toward Grand Junction for 21 miles. Take exit 285 south. Beware! It is a very sharp turn so go slowly! Drive south approximately 7 miles to South Turkey Creek Road. Exit to the right, cross under 285 and the entrance is right in front of you. The exit is 1/2 mile before you reach the little town of Aspen Park.
Trailer Parking: Long, drive-through, gravel parking lot but without designated trailer parking.

143

Fees: none
Water: No
Restrooms: Yes, a little way up the hill
Length of Ride: 3.8 miles of trails
Hazards: Hikers, bikers, dogs on leashes.

Description of our ride: We discovered this area quite by accident. We had set out to go to Reynolds Park and noticed this area from Hwy. 285. So we stopped driving and unloaded the horses! We rode up the hill past the restrooms and the picnic area. We took Lodgepole Loop to the left and up the hill. We turned left again onto Sunny Aspen Trail. Near the top of the ridge we turned left onto Ski Run Trail. It makes a loop at the end and comes back. Coming back down on Ski Run Trail, we turned left again onto Sunny Aspen and left onto Lodgepole Loop. This brought us around to the picnic area where we stopped and had lunch. We rode this on a beautiful fall day and this trail took us through dense timber and bright aspen. It is a short ride but worth the effort! The trail is clearly marked. It is rocky only in a few places. It would be okay for horses who are not shod though better with shoes. Moderate conditioning would be needed.

Meyers Ranch was first homesteaded in 1870 by Duncan McIntyre. He sold the land in 1883 to Louis Ramboz who built the present ranch house. Mr. Ramboz used the land to run cattle and harvest hay and timber. An interesting legend is that the land was used as the winter home for animals from the P.T. Barnum Circus in the late 1880's. When Norman Meyer, was remodeling the ranch house in 1995, he found a board with the inscription: "Circus Town, 1889." So, there seems to be some validity to the legend. In the 1940's, part of the Meyer's Ranch Park area was used as a ski hill. Most of that area is now a beautiful aspen grove. Norman F. and Ethel E. Meyer purchased the land in 1950 and used it for grazing and haying. They still reside in the historic Victorian home on the north side of Hwy. 285 and appreciate their privacy.

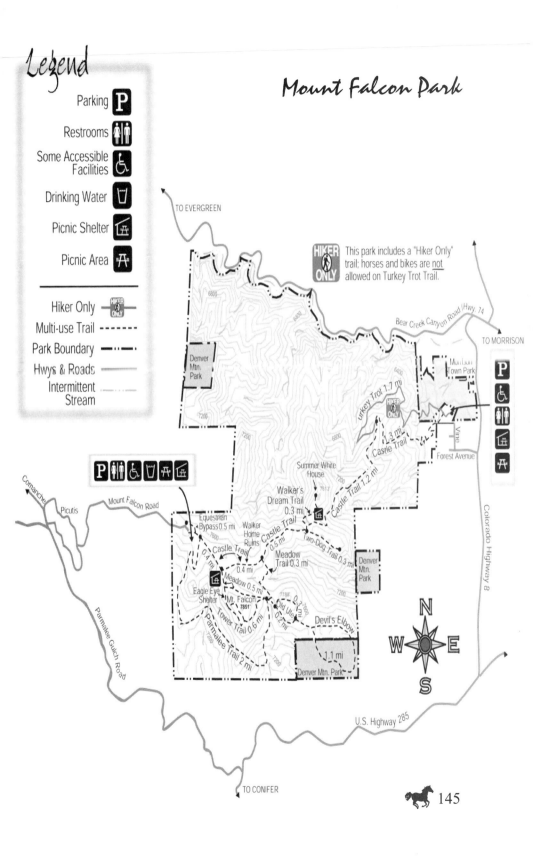

Legend

Parking **P**

Restrooms

Some Accessible Facilities

Drinking Water

Picnic Shelter

Picnic Area

Hiker Only

Multi-use Trail

Park Boundary

Hwys & Roads

Intermittent Stream

Mount Falcon Park

TO EVERGREEN

HIKER ONLY This park includes a "Hiker Only" trail; horses and bikes are not allowed on Turkey Trot Trail.

Bear Creek Canyon Road (Hwy. 74)

TO MORRISON

Denver Mtn. Park

Morrison Town Park

Vine

Forest Avenue

6800

6800

7200

6800

6400

Turkey Trot 1.7 mi

1.3 mi

Castle Trail

Summer White House

Castle Trail 1.2 mi

Colorado Highway 8

Comanche

Picutis

Mount Falcon Road

Walker's Dream Trail 0.3 mi

Equestrian Bypass 0.5 mi

Walker Home Ruins

Castle Trail

0.5 mi

Two-Dog Trail 0.3 mi

Denver Mtn. Park

0.4 mi

Castle Trail

0.4 mi

Meadow Trail 0.3 mi

Meadow 0.5 mi

Eagle Eye Shelter

Mt. Falcon 7851'

Old Ute

0.2 mi

0.2 mi

Devil's Elbow

Parmalee Gulch Road

Tower Trail 0.6 mi

Parmalee Trail 2 mi

1.1 mi

Denver Mtn. Park

N W E S

U.S. Highway 285

TO CONIFER

145

Mount Falcon Park - Jefferson County

Travel Distance: 30.7 miles
Travel Time: 39 minutes
Travel Directions: From Lincoln, go north on I-25 for 0.9 miles to the C-470 exit going west. Go west on C-470 for 21 miles to the 285 exit going west. Go very slowly around this exit. Drive west on 285 for 4.3 miles to Parmalee Gulch Road. Turn right and follow Parmalee Gulch for 2.7 miles to Picutis Road. Turn right and then an immediate left onto Comanchee Road. Follow the signs for another 1.8 miles to the Park.

Trailer Parking: There is a large paved lot at the top of the hill divided into two sections. I would recommend the first lot. Even though it may be farther from the restrooms, it has been completely free of cars every time we went there.
Note: There is a second trailhead and parking lot at the base of the mountain for those who would like extra conditioning by making the steep climb up Castle Trail. This large gravel parking lot is found by taking Colorado 8 north from Morrison to Forest Avenue. Go west on Forest Avenue to Vine.

Follow Vine down the hill and through the rural neighborhood until you find the large gravel parking lot.

Fees: None
Water: No
Restrooms: Yes, very nice but locked in the winter.
Length of Ride: We covered all the upper trails in 2.5 hours
Hazards: Hikers, dogs on leashes, mountain bikes. The Parmelee Gulch Trail has a few step-over water crossings in the spring. The Castle Trail is a bit rocky in places but not too bad.

Description of our ride: This park has special meaning to the Riding Colorado Test Riders. It was our excitement at finding this trail that led us to the idea to write this book and share our "finds" with other equestrians. We keep bringing new people to see this beautiful park and have visited it every season of the year. It is always a treat and especially nice because it is so close. On the day of this writing, we started our ride going down the hill on the Parmelee Gulch Trail. We were greeted by a huge flock of wild turkeys. Here we had beautiful views of the Hwy. 285 valley. We rode through open areas and wooded areas as we descended and ascended. We then took the Tower Trail through the trees to the Meadow Trail. Here we turned right and rode east to the Ute Trail and Devil's Elbow Trail, both of which are loops that bring you back to the Meadow Trail. We then rode north on the Meadow Trail to where it connects with the Castle Trail. We turned right and went to visit the castle ruins and the foundation for the President's summer home. You must get off your horse and spend a minute reading the history of these historic sites. It is so interesting! As we rode back we enjoyed the views of the Denver area, Red Rocks and the mountains to the west. We then rode up the 2-Dog Trail to its end, enjoyed the view and rode back. On our way back west to the parking lot, we came upon a large herd of deer and watched two Bald Eagles circling above us. Most of the trail is packed dirt although the Castle Trail, both at the top and down to the lower parking lot, has some loose rocky places.

Shoes would not be required, however.

This park is part of the 4,000 acres once owned by businessman John Brisben Walker. The Castle Trail was once a road used by the Stanley Steamer Autos, a company purchased by Walker that lost out to the Model T. Mr. Walker built his dream house, a unique stone castle, in the early 1900's only to see it burn down in 1918. His dream of a summer white house for the presidents didn't get past the foundation stones. One dream that was realized, however, was Red

Rocks Amphitheater.

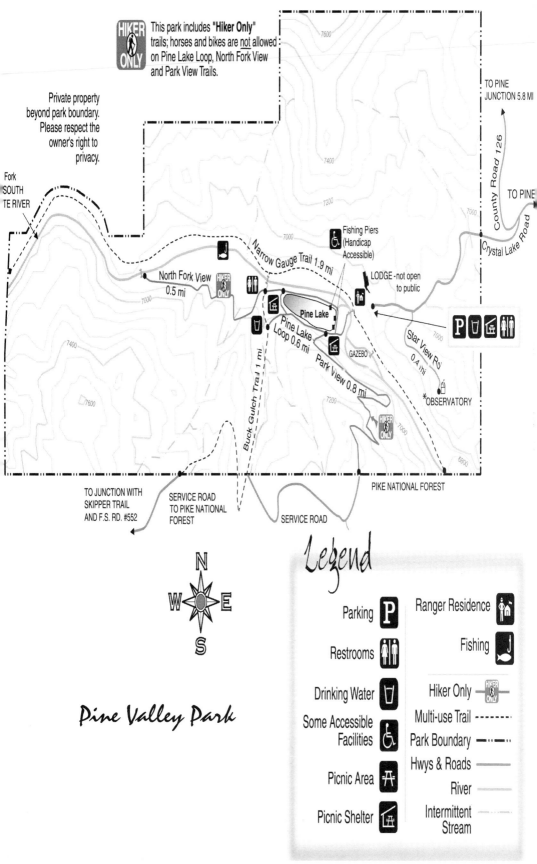

HIKER ONLY
This park includes "Hiker Only" trails; horses and bikes are not allowed on Pine Lake Loop, North Fork View and Park View Trails.

TO PINE JUNCTION 5.8 MI

Private property beyond park boundary. Please respect the owner's right to privacy.

County Road 126

TO PINE

Crystal Lake Road

Fork SOUTH TE RIVER

7600

7400

7200

7000

Narrow Gauge Trail 1.9 mi

Fishing Piers (Handicap Accessible)

North Fork View 0.5 mi

HIKER ONLY

LODGE - not open to public

Pine Lake

P

Pine Lake Loop 0.6 mi

Park View 0.8 mi

Star View Rd 0.4 mi

GAZEBO

Buck Gulch Trail 1 mi

7400

7600

7200

7000

HIKER ONLY

*OBSERVATORY

6800

PIKE NATIONAL FOREST

TO JUNCTION WITH SKIPPER TRAIL AND F.S. RD. #552

SERVICE ROAD TO PIKE NATIONAL FOREST

SERVICE ROAD

N
W E
S

Pine Valley Park

Legend

Parking	P	Ranger Residence	
Restrooms		Fishing	
Drinking Water		Hiker Only	HIKER ONLY
Some Accessible Facilities		Multi-use Trail	------
		Park Boundary	—··—··—
Picnic Area		Hwys & Roads	——
		River	
Picnic Shelter		Intermittent Stream	

Pine Valley Park - Jefferson County

Travel Distance: 42.1 miles
Travel Time: 1 hour
Travel Directions: From Lincoln, go north on I-25 for 0.9 miles to the C-470 exit going west. Go west on C-470 for 21 miles to the 285 exit going west. Drive west on 285 for 21.4 miles to Pine Junction. Go south on Hey. 126 for 6 miles. Take a sharp right onto Crystal Lake Road. Drive 0.5 miles to the entrance and drive another 0.5 miles to the parking lot.

Trailer Parking: There is a large paved lot with lines painted for 10 trailers. The lower lot is for cars.
Fees: None
Water: Yes, down by the picnic areas along the river.
Restrooms: Yes, very nice
Length of Ride: We rode for 3 hours, counting a 1/2 hour stop for lunch, at a relaxed pace and covered 6 miles.
Hazards: You must cross a bridge to get up to the mountain

trail and the national park access, hikers, dogs on leashes, very popular with mountain bikers.

Description of our ride: The Narrow Gauge Trail, along the North Fork of the South Platte River, is very beautiful, flat and wide. The total distance of this trail which runs the length of the park is 1.9 miles and would be a lovely, easy ride for beginners or out of condition horses. We chose to cross the bridge and ride up into the mountains on the Buck Gulch Trail. This trail wove through the High Meadow Fire damage that took place in approximately 2000. It is amazing how slowly the forest recovers from a fire. As we rode through the park in 2004, only mountain grasses and a few wildflowers had returned. The trail goes back and forth between the burn and the lush forest and up and down ridges. The trail is about 1 mile long and ends up leaving the park and connecting with the Skipper Trail in the Pike National Forest. The Skipper Trail is a beautiful trail that follows along a creek. We rode quite a long way down this trail before turning around.

The Pine Valley Ranch was originally homesteaded in 1908 by J. Hildebrand and used as a cattle ranch. In 1927, a later owner, William A. Baehr, had the mountain lodge built in only ninety days by a work crew of sixty craftsmen working around the clock. The Baehr Lodge is a beautiful example of a German Black Forest manor home. The lodge is not currently open to the public although it was purchased with the rest of the park in 1986 by Jefferson County Open space.

Shoes would not be required but conditioning is. The climb up Buck Gulch Trail left our horses breathing hard.

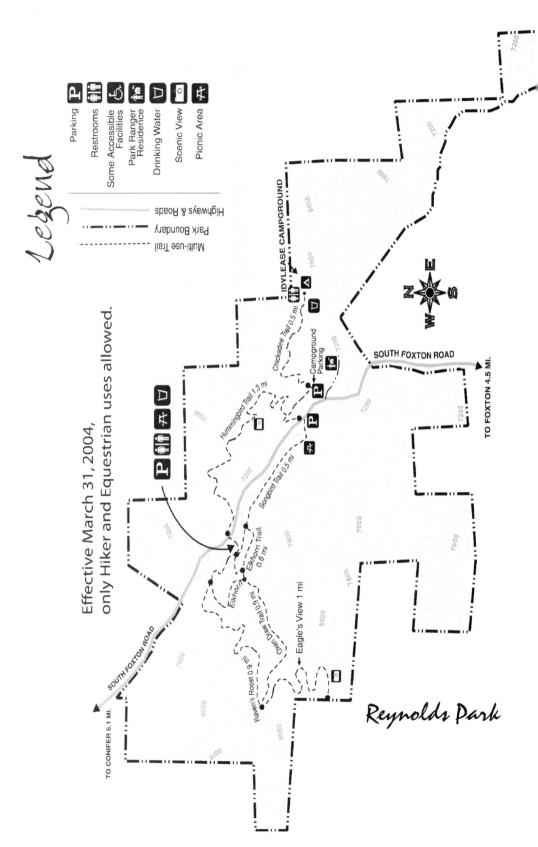

Legend

Parking
Restrooms
Some Accessible Facilities
Park Ranger Residence
Drinking Water
Scenic View
Picnic Area

Highways & Roads
Park Boundary
Multi-use Trail

Effective March 31, 2004, only Hiker and Equestrian uses allowed.

IDYLEASE CAMPGROUND

Chickadee Trail/0.5 mi

Hummingbird Trail 1.3 mi

Campground Parking

SOUTH FOXTON ROAD

Songbird Trail 0.5 mi

TO FOXTON 4.5 MI.

Elkhorn Trail

Elkhorn Trail 0.8 mi

Elkhorn

Oxen Draw Trail 0.9 mi

Raven's Roost 0.9 mi

Eagle's View 1 mi

SOUTH FOXTON ROAD

TO CONIFER 5.1 MI.

Reynolds Park

Reynolds Park -
Jefferson County Open Space

Travel Distance: 43 miles
Travel Time: 50 min.
Travel Directions: Go North on I-25 for 0.9 miles. Exit onto C-470 going west toward Grand Junction for 21 miles. Take the exit onto Hwy. 285 south. Beware! It is a very sharp turn so go slowly! Go 15 miles. Just past Conifer look for the signs to Reynolds Park. You will take a right hand exit onto Foxton Road. This exit is right after a sharp turn so watch for the brown sign. You will then go under the highway. At the stop sign, go left, staying on Foxton Road. Go 5 miles. The largest parking lot is on your right. There is a smaller lot a little farther down on your right and another lot farther down on your left for the campers.

Trailer Parking: There is a large gravel lot that can hold several trailers. However, trailer spots are not specifically marked off. The west parking lots both have picnic tables. The larger lot also has a water pump and clean restrooms.

Fees: none unless camping

Water: Yes, pump and creek

Restrooms: Yes

Length of Ride: 5.9 miles of trails

Hazards: Oxen Draw trail zig-zags back and forth over a small stream. Trails also used by hikers, and dogs on leashes. You might see wildlife, we saw a herd of 75 elk on one trip. You will have to cross Foxton Road to get to the eastern side of the park.

Description of our ride: We started our ride by the picnic area. We rode south to the intersection of Songbird Trail and Elkhorn Trail. We turned right and rode up Elkhorn Trail then took a left onto Oxen Draw Trail. During the spring and early summer this trail cris-crosses a small stream several times. Since one of my horses is a jumper and doesn't like water, we did lots of jumping! In the fall, the stream was dry. We rode up the hill and turned left onto Eagle's View. This is a dead-end trail but worth the ride. It ends at the top of the ridge and gives you breathtaking views. After taking some pictures, we turned around and rode back down to the intersection with the other trails. We turned left onto Raven's Roost and followed it around and down to the picnic area. This entire loop was very forested with the exception of the meadow at the top of Eagle's View.We then crossed Foxton Road in the middle of the parking lot and started up the hill on Hummingbird Trail. Here we were presented with an entirely different type of terrain for most of the trail. It was rockier and more open. The trail climbs sharply and you soon find yourself looking way down on the road below. The loop curves over a ridge and back south connecting with the small parking lot and picnic area. Before crossing back over the street, we took a left at the sign that pointed to the campground. We rode up Chickadee Trail to the camp sites. We found a beautiful, secluded, campground with 5 campsites, one of which is set up with a hitching post. This campground must be reached by horse or foot so you must pack everything in along the 0.5 mile trail. There is water and a restroom. Reservations can be made three days ahead. We then rode back to the Hummingbird Trail, crossed the street and rode the Songbird Trail back to the large parking lot. This figure eight ride was a wonderful half day adventure through a variety of terrain. I would recommend shoes as parts are a bit rocky. Your horse needs to be in good condition as some of the climbs are quite steep.

Reynolds Park is named after John A. Reynolds who once owned a large part of the park. This park was dedicated in 1977. It seems to be an under-used gem, however, as I have been there for three trail rides and have seen only one or two other users. This park is on land that was one of the first areas settled in Colorado. It was a rest stop for pack trains traveling between Leadville and Denver. For nearly 30 years in the early 1900's it was a dude ranch with fourteen cabins. The Reynolds family home served as the main lodge and the family's residence. The Reynolds family donated a substantial part of the park to Jefferson County.

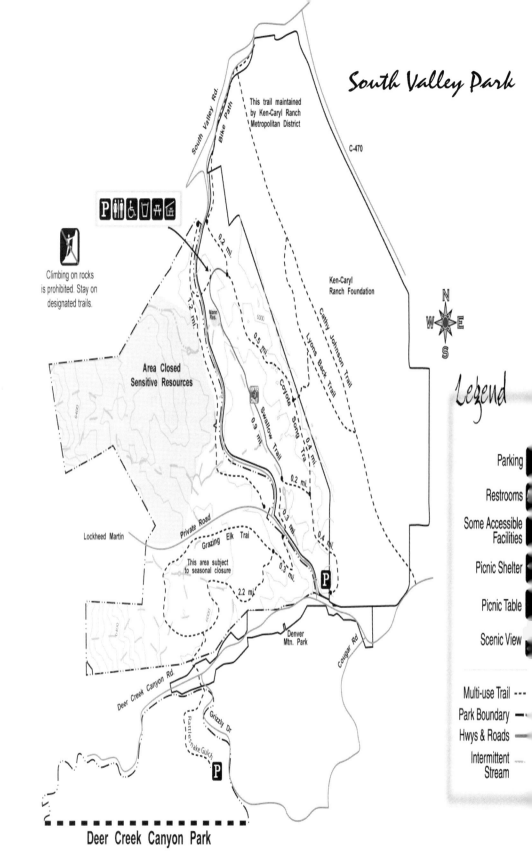

South Valley Park - Jefferson County

Travel Distance: 18.5 miles
Travel Time: 22 minutes
Travel Directions: From Lincoln, go north on I-25 for 0.9 miles to the C-470 exit going west. Go west on C-470 for 16.2 miles to the Ken Caryl Exit. Go West on Ken Caryl Parkway for 0.4 miles. At the light, go left on South Valley Road. The entrance to the park is 1 mile south on your left.

Trailer Parking: There is a large paved lot with designated trailer parking on the south side. There is room for 3 trailers here. More room is available if the lot is not full, especially during the week.
Fees: None
Water: Yes
Restrooms: Yes, very nice
Length of Ride: We rode for 3 hours, counting a 1/2 hour stop for lunch, at a rather fast pace and covered 7 miles.
Hazards: Hikers, dogs on leashes, mountain bikers, road

crossing if you want to go to Grazing Elk Trail, Valley View Trail, or to take Rattlesnake Gulch Trail over to Deer Creek Canyon Park. Stairs at the parking lot and at Lyons Back Trail.

Description of our ride: Wow, Wow, Wow! This park will wow you! The red rock formations and the valley views are so beautiful! We went in August and because of the cool, wet summer, there were wild flowers in abundance! The main part of the trail is wide packed sand and just perfect for any horse or rider. We left the parking lot by climbing up the stairs to get on the Coyote Song Trail. We rode south on this trail all the way to the south parking lot after taking a detour up the Lyons Back Trail. Exploring the Ken Caryl Open Space from this trail would be a fun ride in and of itself! After reaching the south parking lot, we cut back 0.4 of a mile to the cut through that would take us to the Grazing Elk Trail. (This trail is closed at times during the fall if a herd of elk is present.) To get to this trail, you have to cross the wide road that leads to Lockheed-Martin. It is not terribly busy but people do drive fast along it. Once across, we followed a narrow dirt and somewhat rocky trail up the hill to the meadow. We took the loop in a clockwise direction to the Rattlesnake Gulch Trail. We went down the trail to where it ends at Deer Creek Canyon Road. We crossed the road and rode a short distance east before crossing a bridge to get to the trail that takes you up into Deer Creek Canyon Park. (See the evaluation for Deer Creek Canyon Park.) You could ride for hours if you did both of these parks at once! We cut back across the road, up Rattlesnake Gulch and continued on the Grazing Elk Trail loop in a clockwise direction and back to the parking lot along Coyote Song Trail. We rode at a fast pace, trotting and cantering a lot and covered over 7 miles.

This beautiful park is 909 acres and was acquired from Lockheed-Martin in 1999. It had originally been owned by Frank Mann and was purchased by John Shaffer, the founder of Ken-Caryl, in 1926. Johns-Manville Corporation constructed its headquarters on the site in 1971. These headquarters later became Martin Marietta which is now Lockheed-Martin.

Several day trips could be taken at this one site. You could just stay in the main park and ride the Coyote Song Trail and enjoy the beautiful scenery. You could include the Grazing Elk Trail. You could go over the ridge on the Lyon's Back Trail and ride the Cathy Johnson and Columbine Trail in the Ken-Caryl Open Space or you could ride clear into Deer Creek Canyon Park for a very long ride.

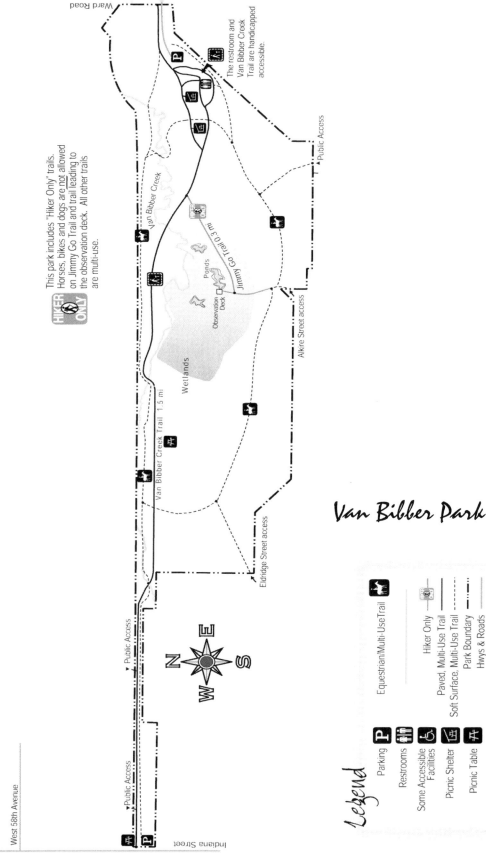

Van Bibber Park

West 58th Avenue

Ward Road

Indiana Street

Van Bibber Creek

Wetlands

Ponds

Observation Deck

Van Bibber Creek Trail 1.5 mi

Jimmy Go Trail 0.3 mi

Public Access

Eldridge Street access

Alkire Street access

This park includes "Hiker Only" trails. Horses, bikes and dogs are <u>not</u> allowed on Jimmy Go Trail and trail leading to the observation deck. All other trails are multi-use.

HIKER ONLY

The restroom and Van Bibber Creek Trail are handicapped accessible.

N E S W

Legend

Parking

Restrooms

Some Accessible Facilities

Picnic Shelter

Picnic Table

Interpretive Signage

Equestrian/Multi-Use Trail

Hiker Only

Paved, Multi-Use Trail

Soft Surface, Multi-Use Trail

Park Boundary

Hwys & Roads

Creek

Van Bibber Park - Jefferson County

Travel Distance: 30 miles
Travel Time: 42 minutes
Travel Directions: From Lincoln, go north on I-25 for 20.9 miles to the I-70 interchange. Go west on I-70 for 8 miles to the Ward Road Exit. Go north on Ward Road for 1.2 miles. The Park entrance is on the west side of the road but you cannot enter from the north-bound lane. You will have to go up to 58th and turn around in the gas station. Head back south on Ward and go into the parking lot.

Trailer Parking: Large paved lot with designated trailer parking for three trailers. The parking lot on the West side of the park off Indiana is smaller but could also fit several trailers.
Fees: None
Water: Yes
Restrooms: Yes, very nice.
Length of Ride: We rode for 1 hour and 25 minutes

including a twenty minute stop for lunch at a lovely picnic table under an umbrella of tree limbs. We covered 3.5 miles.

Hazards: Hikers, dogs on leashes, bikers. One section of the trail that goes to the west end goes along the backyards of some lovely homes so plan on anything!

Description of our ride: This is a lovely, peaceful park right in the middle of Arvada. The Van Bibber Creek Trail, going west along the north end of the park, is 1.5 miles of easy, almost level riding. We were trotting along when we came to a beautiful spot for lunch. We then rode to the west edge of the park. It ends at Indiana Street. However, plans are in place to build a trail that would connect this park with White Ranch Park. Coming back, we took the trail that goes south and up the hill. The trail was wide and sandy along here and was great for a long canter!

This park has an interesting history. The first recorded gold strike was made on nearby Ralston Creek in 1850. The fertile land became home to many crops once irrigation canals were dug. By 1870, there were around 500 residents in the little farming community of Arvada.

Note: We rode the trails at Crown Hill Park and Van Bibber Park on the same day. To get to Van Bibber Park from Crown Hill, simply drive north on Kipling to 58th then west on 58th to Ward Road. Turn left on Ward Road and right into park entrance.

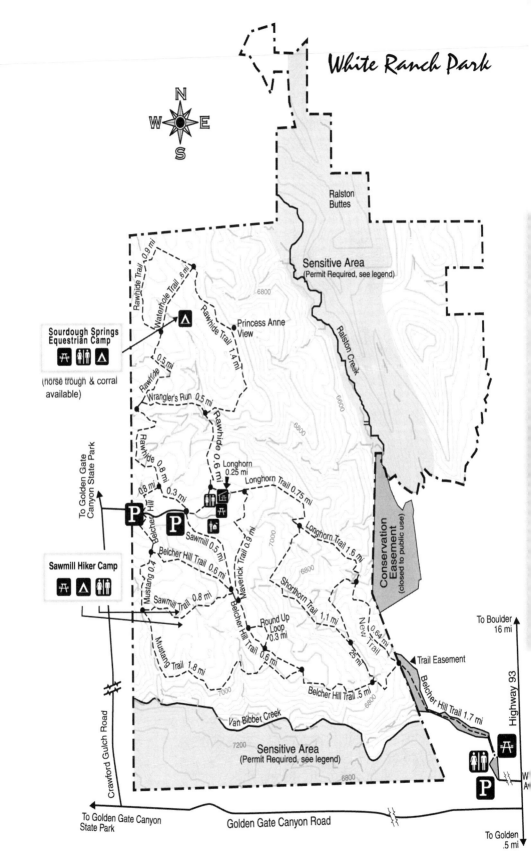

White Ranch Park

Ralston Buttes

Sensitive Area
(Permit Required, see legend)

Rawhide Trail 0.9 mi

Waterhole Trail .6 mi

Rawhide Trail 1.4 mi

Princess Anne View

Ralston Creek

6800

Sourdough Springs
Equestrian Camp

(horse trough & corral available)

0.5 mi

Rawhide

Wrangler's Run 0.5 mi

Rawhide 0.6 mi

6600

6800

6800

Longhorn 0.25 mi

Longhorn Trail 0.75 mi

Longhorn Trail 1.6 mi

Rawhide 0.8 mi

0.8 mi

0.3 mi

To Golden Gate Canyon State Park

Belcher Hill

Sawmill 0.5 mi

Belcher Hill Trail 0.6 mi

Maverick Trail 0.9 mi

7000

Conservation Easement
(closed to public use)

Sawmill Hiker Camp

Mustang 0.7

Sawmill Trail 0.8 mi

Belcher Hill Trail 0.6 mi

Round Up Loop 0.3 mi

6800

Shorthorn Trail 1.1 mi

New Trail

0.64 mi

To Boulder 16 mi

Mustang Trail 1.8 mi

.25 mi

Trail Easement

7000

Belcher Hill Trail .5 mi

6800

Belcher Hill Trail 1.7 mi

Highway 93

Van Bibber Creek

7200

Sensitive Area
(Permit Required, see legend)

6800

W A

Crawford Gulch Road

To Golden Gate Canyon
State Park

Golden Gate Canyon Road

To Golden
.5 mi

White Ranch - Jefferson County

Travel Distance: 42.1 miles
Travel Time: 1 hour
Travel Directions: From Lincoln, go north on I-25 for 0.9 miles to the C-470 exit going west. Go west on C-470 for 26.2 miles to the I-70 junction. Stay to the left toward Grand Junction but do not get onto I-70. Continue straight toward Golden on Hwy. 6. Proceed west for 4.5 miles to the signal. Go through the light onto Hwy. 93 for 1.4 miles to Golden Gate Canyon Drive. Turn left. Drive 3.9 miles to Crawford Gulch Road. Turn right and drive a windy 3.8 miles to the park entrance. Follow the road to the end to find the trailer parking in a large lot on the left.

Trailer Parking: Large designated trailer parking, room for several trailers. Gravel parking lot with easy turn around. Picnic tables. There is a large corral-round pen.
Fees: None
Water: Yes, but shut off during the winter.

 164

Restrooms: Yes

Length of Ride: We rode for 3.5 hours, counting a 1/2 hour stop for lunch, at a fast pace and covered 9.2 miles.

Hazards: A few small water crossings. Hikers, dogs on leashes, bikers, wildlife.

Description of our ride: Get your "ooh's and aah's" ready for this one! What a fabulous park! The views of the City of Denver and the mountains were unbelievable! The parking lot is in the middle so you could easily make two different rides out of this one by riding to the north one day and to the south another. I really couldn't tell you which was more beautiful as both sides were spectacular! We rode at a rather fast clip as there

were only three of us that day and we wanted to explore both sides. At the parking area there is a fun outdoor museum of old farm equipment. Nancy claimed she could remember using tools like that! We started to the north on the Rawhide Trail and followed it clear around to the Sourdough Springs Equestrian Campground. What a find! We went back during the summer for an overnight with all the test riders. This is a beautiful campground with 8 sites. All the sites have hitching posts and sites 1-4 have two corrals. There is a nice brick outhouse and firewood and buckets are provided. There is water but you must pack in everything else. Camping sites are available by permit only so you need to contact Jefferson County

Open Space at 303-271-5925 for more information. After exploring the campground, we rode back to the parking lot on the remaining section of the Rawhide Trail which is along the campground service road at this point. We then rode to the south side of the park on the Sawmill Trail to the Sawmill hiker campground. We stopped here at a picnic table for lunch. We continued west to the Mustang Trail which takes you downhill and over a few small water crossings. We turned

 left at the Belcher Hill Trail and right onto the Maverick Trail and left onto the Longhorn Trail which takes you back to the parking lot. There are lots of other trails still to be ridden in this park!

This land was once part of the Ute and Arapaho tribes hunting area. In 1865 James and Mary Bond from Wales were on their way to California when their little boy was killed under the wheels of their wagon. So the heartbroken couple stopped where they were and settled here. Their home is still on the park property. Around 1913, Paul and Anna Lee White purchased a portion of the property and it was their large gift that allowed the park land to be purchased.

RIDING COLORADO

LARIMER COUNTY

North Fork Trail-Roosevelt National Forest to Rocky Mountain National Park- Larimer County

Travel Distance: 92.7 miles
Travel Time: 2 hours and 15 minutes
Travel Directions: Go north on I-25 for 63.8 miles to Hwy. 34 (exit # 257B). This is a sharp exit so slow down! Go west, toward Loveland on Hwy. 34 for 20.7 miles to Drake. When the road splits, veer to the right toward Glen Haven (Hwy. 43.) Drive for 6.1 miles to County Road 51 B, Dunraven Glade. Turn right and follow this little road for 2.1 miles to

the trailhead on your left.

Trailer Parking: An open gravel area is available with plenty of room for several trailers.

Fees: None

Water: None at the trailhead but the trail follows the North Fork of the Big Thompson River for quite a way and you cross it many times so the horses can get water from there.

Restroom: Yes, outhouse

Length of Ride: 10.6 miles but you can go forever into Rocky Mountain National Park. It took us nearly 4 hours to complete our ride.

Hazards: Hikers, bikers, dogs on leashes, some rocky areas, large river crossings or bridges, underground springs leave muddy areas in some parts of the trail. The forest service requests that you go through the mud, not around it.

Description of our ride: We gave this ride a 10! We started out from the trailhead following the trail toward Lost Lake in Rocky Mountain National Park. We crossed the North Fork of the Big Thompson River several times. We passed Camp Cheley, a youth summer camp, now closed for the winter, and continued on up the trail. You will also pass a lot of wilderness camping areas along the way. Once you enter Rocky Mountain National Park the trail really begins to climb so don't bring out-of-condition horses. This is a tough trail in places though not dangerous. The vistas and river crossings make this a wonderful ride. We turned around at the 5.6 mile maker in the park. It was another 4.4 miles to Lost Lake. That would be a fun destination if you get an early start and your horse is ready for it. We loved this ride. I would recommend shoes.

Roosevelt National Forest is on the eastern side of the Continental Divide and was named the Colorado National Forest in 1910. Its name was changed in 1932 by President Herbert Hoover to honor President Theodore Roosevelt.

RIDING COLORADO

PARK COUNTY

Kenosha Pass - Park County

Travel Distance: 69.2 miles
Travel Time: 1 hour 20 minutes
Travel Directions: Go north on I-25 for just under a mile to the C-470 west exit. Drive for 21 miles west on C-470 to the 285 south exit (Fairplay.) Be careful, this is a sharp turn off of this exit. Drive south on 285 for 47.3 miles. The day-use picnic area is on your left.

Trailer Parking: Parking is available for free along both sides of 285 in the wide gravel areas or along the sides of the access road to the picnic area. If you park within the picnic area, there is a $4 fee. The picnic area is a bit tight for trailers, however.
Fees: $4 if you park within the picnic area.
Water: Yes, at the campground area on the west side of 285
Restroom: Yes, outhouse
Length of Ride: Kenosha Pass is an access for the Colorado Trail so you can go for days in either direction from this point.

171

We stayed on the east side of 285 and picked up the trail going southeast. We rode for 3.5 miles then turned around and came back. It took us 3 hours.

Hazards: Hikers and bikers, loose rocks, wildlife.

Description of our ride: If you ever wonder why you live in Colorado, just come to Kenosha Pass in September! We went here on a beautiful fall day just at the height of the Aspen season. The trees were absolutely aglow! Not only were the trees amazing but the views of the South Park Valley area were breathtaking as well. This was well worth the drive! The trail is a gentle climb but remember that you are starting at nearly 10,000 feet. So, have your horse in condition or go slowly. I would recommend shoes as there were several rocky places that were hard to tip-toe through. We stopped for lunch at the top of a ridge where there was still plenty of grass due to our wet summer. From that point, we had views to the east, south and west. You will really be thrilled with this ride! The trail is narrow in spots and either dirt or loose rocks.

The Colorado Trail goes west from the campground side of Kenosha Pass. Another great ride would be to go west for about 6 miles to the Beaver Ponds Picnic Ground.

Kenosha Pass is a popular area for ATV's. Fortunately, they are not allowed on the Colorado Trail so you will not have a problem with them.

RIDING COLORADO

TELLER COUNTY

173

Dome Rock Trail - Teller County

Travel Distance: 78.4 miles

Travel Time: 1 hour 45 minutes

Travel Directions: Go south on I-25 for 52.5 miles to Hwy. 24 (exit # 141 - Cimarron St.) Go west for 18.5 miles, through Woodland Park to Divide. When the road splits, veer to the left toward Mueller State Park and Cripple Creek (Hwy. 67). Drive for 5.4 miles, passing the entrance to Mueller State Park to County Road 61 which veers of to your right. This road is easy to miss as it looks like a private entrance with upright logs on either side and a sign that reads "Rainbow Valley Ranch." Turn right and follow this little road, which becomes dirt, for 2.0 miles to the trailhead on your right. You will have to go down a steep hill to get to the parking lot. Make sure your brakes work, One horseman rolled a big rig on this drive-way! You will enter to the right then make an immediate left turn so go slowly!

Trailer Parking: An open gravel area is available with plenty of room for many trailers.

Fees: none

Water: There is a water pump at the east side of the parking lot. The trail crosses Fourmile Creek many times so the horses can also get water from there.

Restroom: Yes, outhouse

Length of Ride: 9.4 miles

Hazards: Hikers, wildlife, river crossings. No dogs or bikers are allowed.

Description of our ride: On a scale of 1 to 10 this ride is a 15! This ride gives you everything from beautiful views of Pikes Peak and the Continental Divide to gorgeous rides through aspen groves and evergreens and deep river crossings. You will also be thrilled with the beauty of the of huge granite rock formations, especially Dome Rock itself which rises 800 feet above the canyon floor. We started our ride at the west parking lot on the Willow Creek Trail #40 and rode for three miles up a gentle slope on a packed sand two-lane trail. After about three miles, the trail narrows to single file and shortly thereafter we came to a "Y" in the trail. We took the right branch, up a steep climb. At the highest view point we were at 9,700 feet, which is a long way up from the parking lot which was at 8,800 feet. The views of the mountains and the aspens were bright yellow on this sunny October day. We then continued on this trail, passing the Sand Creek Trail #41 on the right which is a great short cut if you need a shorter ride. We turned off onto Spring Creek Trail #43 and followed it all the way to Dome Rock. The trail makes some steep drops as it approaches Dome Rock but nothing that was a problem. Just as we rode past the south side of Dome Rock we had our first water crossing. It was deep and wide but the bottom of the river was sandy so very easy to cross. We had lunch in the meadow by the rock. We then circled around the rock on Dome Rock Trail #46. This trail takes you back and forth over Fourmile Creek nine times. It also takes you into Mueller State Park at some points. About 2.5 miles from the end, we came across the ruins of Jackrabbit

Lodge. This had been a private hunting lodge that burned to the ground in the 1940's. All that remains is the stone chimney and part of the foundation.

At this lodge you can choose to go left into Mueller State Park. We continued on the Dome Rock Trail having fun crossing the river and viewing the herd of Big Horn Sheep that live there. River crossings can be avoided by staying on the north side of the river along the footpath. We stayed on the wide road, that was once a stage coach road, and had fun playing in the water. At times the river was so deep from the beaver dams that the water came above our horses' bellies! About 0.5 miles from the end we came across the ruins of an old collapsed mine. This trail returns to the east end of the parking lot. This is an easy trail and shoes would not be required as the surface is packed sand.

Note: This complete 9.4 mile loop is only open from July 16th to November 30th. It is closed for the rest of the year for the Big Horn Sheep lambing. But you can take shorter loops, such as the Sand Creek Trail loop, or going out and back on the Willow Creek Trail or the Dome Rock Trail.

Mueller State Park - Teller County

Travel Distance: 74.8 miles
Travel Time: 1 hour and 40 minutes
Travel Directions: Go south on I-25 for 52.5 miles to Hwy. 24 (exit # 141 - Cimarron St.) Go west for 18.5 miles, through Woodland Park to Divide. When the road splits, veer to the left toward Mueller State Park and Cripple Creek (Hwy. 67). Drive for 3.8 miles to the entrance to Mueller State Park on your right. You will have to stop at the gatehouse to pay your fee and get a trail map. The park ranger will give you directions to the trailer parking which is by the stables.

Trailer Parking: There is a large paved parking lot by the stables with painted spots for 12 trailers.
Fees: $5.00
Water: There is a water pump by the stables but it was turned off when we were there.

Restroom: Yes, it is across the road and up the hill.
Length of Ride: We rode for 4.5 hours and covered 10 miles
Hazards: Part of the park is open for hunting beginning in October so check at the gate to find out where those boundaries are located. Hikers, wildlife, school kids on a field trip. No dogs or bikers are allowed

Description of our ride: Mueller State Park was once part of the real wild west! It was the hiding place of moonshiners and outlaws. Today it is still as wild and untamed covering 12,000 acres of meadows, granite formations, aspen and pine groves, and wildlife. There are 80 miles of trails, many of which are open to horses. Added to that are the trails that connect to the state wildlife areas. The trails are a maze so you could take many day trips and not see the same parts of the park. They are also a bit confusing so take your map along with you. Trails that are open only to hikers are fairly clearly marked.

We started our ride by taking the Livery Trail #20 up the hill on the northeast side of the parking lot. This connected us to the Elk Meadow Trail #18. This trail takes you through a big open meadow with beautiful views of the west side of Pikes Peak. At the bottom of a hill you will come to the Cheesman Ranch Trail #17. We went to the right. The first part of this trail goes along Hwy. 67 so you do have some traffic that is visible. If your horse is afraid of trucks and cars, take note. We continued north on this trail as it climbed up a hill. At the crest of the hill, just before we entered the forest, we came across the ruins of an old dug out root seller. The parks people tell you not to dig around in the old buildings as you might encounter a rat! We rode down the hill through the trees to the Cheesman Ranch. Here you will see a picturesque log cabin, an old barn and fences. Beyond the barn is another ranch house. We followed the Cheesman Ranch Trail in a large loop until we came to Homestead Trail #12 going to the right. This is a beautiful wooded part of the park. We rode to the point where trail #12 becomes a hiker only trail and were forced onto Logger Trail #31 for a short distance. This trail took us briefly into the hunting area which we didn't like. So, we rode quickly and made a lot of noise! We were glad to be wearing our red "Riding Colorado" jackets! This trail takes you to an intersection with #13 to your right or #25 to your left. We went left onto Black Bear Trail #25 which changes its name to Geer Pond at the intersection with #28. This trail takes you by both Geer Pond and Lost Pond and loops you back to the stable. This is a large loop and very beautiful.

The trails are easy, wide and packed sand. Shoes would not be required. You can take a much shorter loop by taking the Cheesman Ranch trail #17 to the left and going over to #12 from there. Longer rides can be taken by going right at Nobel Cabin Trail #30 instead of turning left on #25. However, that is the area that is open to hunting some of the year so check with the forest ranger when you enter.

Horses are available for rent at the stables during the summer months. Golden Eagle Outfitters can be reached by calling 719-686-7373. They have a variety of options from 1 hour rides to breakfast or dinner rides.

APPENDIX A
Safety Tips

As we all know, there are inherent risks in horseback riding. Add a horse trailer and a trail and those risks increase...but so does the fun! So, take a minute and read through these safety recommendations. We hope they will make your day trip go more smoothly.

1. Make sure your trailer is in good working order, especially brakes, lights and floor boards.

2. Bring along:
- This book
- Vehicle and trailer registrations
- Cell phone and charger (carry the phone in your pocket during the ride.)
- Spare tires for car and trailer. Chocks, Jack (I like the ramp type,) and tire iron for changing tires (we've needed these three times so far!)
- First-aid kits for humans and horses
- Insect spray for humans and horses
- Water and food for humans and horses (at least one gallon of water per horse.)
- Manure fork. Leave parking lots clean!
- Spare halter and lead rope
- Knife/scissors
- Bailing twine. If you need it you'll be glad you have it!
- Horse Blanket

3. In saddle bags bring: (suggested by Carol Crisp on her web-site: equineexplorer.com)
- Food or snack
- Water
- Pocket knife or multi-tool

- Map of trail
- Compass or GPS
- Waterproof jacket or poncho
- Extra bandana
- Mini first-aid kit for horse and rider.
- Emergency Trail Boot
- Hoof Pick
- Twine
- Whistle or bells

4. Always tell someone where you are going

5. I recommend riding with a helmet, especially on trails.

6. Lions, coyotes and bears, oh my! Actually, don't let the wildlife keep you from riding. We have seen lots of non-aggressive type of wildlife. It is part of the treat of trail riding. We have seen one bear (in Bear Creek Regional Park, no less) but no mountain lions. I have talked to the wildlife specialists at the Colorado Division of Wildlife and at Rocky Mountain National Park. With the exception of one incident in the 1970's when an archery hunter on horseback claimed to have been attacked by a grizzly, the wildlife specialists know of no bear or mountain lion attacks on horses. And don't worry, there are no more grizzlies in Colorado! Smaller animals, like dogs, are in much greater danger than a big horse. But, just to be safe, we always made lots of noise on the trail! We also attached bells to our saddles.

7. Lightning is a real threat in Colorado. If you get caught in a lightning storm, find a low spot away from trees and get off your horse.

8. Remember trail etiquette. While bikers and hikers are supposed to yield to horses, and most are extremely courteous, some just do not know how horses will respond. So, communicate with them by telling them your needs.

9. Wear bright clothing during hunting season.

10. If you come to a burn area, be aware that dead falling trees are a real danger.

11. Know the horses in your group. Keep all horses a safe distance from each other. Horses that kick should have a red ribbon on their tail. Some horses will panic if they feel they are being left behind so watch out for one another.

12. Help us keep the trails open to horses. Leave all parking areas, bridges and paved trails clean.

First Aid Kit for Horses

From PetPlace.com

- Antibacterial soap-(such as Betadine) for cleaning wounds
- Antibiotic Ointment-to put on clean wounds
- Sterile Gauze Sponges and pads
- 2-4 disposable diapers or wrapped sanitary napkins
- Bandages-Ace bandages, 2.5 inch gauze bandage roll, Equine leg bandages
- Adhesive Tape-to keep bandages in place
- 2-4 quilted, padded wraps for under bandages
- Household scissors or pocket knife
- Tweezers
- Chemical Ice Pack
- Rectal Thermometer with Rubbing Alcohol and Lubricant such as K-Y Jelly.

Most tack stores have first aid kits for horses but you may want to add some of the items listed above.

APPENDIX B
Rental Horses

We are including these references as a service to our readers. We do not make any recommendations on a particular rental outfit.

Chatfield State Park:
Chatfield Stables (Located inside the park)
303-933-3636
Trail rides, Day Camps, Riding Club, Boarding

Cherry Creek State Park:
Paint Horse Stables (Located inside the Park)
303-690-8235, www.painthorsestables.com
Trail rides, Day Camps, Riding Club, Lessons, Boarding

Garden of the Gods
Academy Riding Stables
1-888-700-0410 or on line at
www.academyridingstables.com.

Mueller State Park (and area)
Golden Eagle Outfitters (located in the park)
719-686-7373
Trail rides, including breakfast and dinner rides. Ages 8 and up. Late spring and summer only.

Cripple Creek Gold Campground and Horse Company
Trail rides and camping
719-689-0131

McNamara's Ranch
Working guest ranch with year a-round trail rides
719-748-3466, www.mcnamararanch.com

Rocky Mountain National Park Area:

Cowpoke Corner Corral and
Rocky Mountain Gateway Stables
970-586-5890 or 970-586-5269,
www.nationalparkgatewaystables.com

Silver Lane Stables
970-586-4695

Sombrero Ranches - Estes Park Stable
Trail rides and overnighters
970-586-4577, info@sombrero.com

APPENDIX C
Contact Numbers

These are the contact numbers for the trails in this book.

City Parks:
Colorado Springs: 719-385-5940
Lakewood: 303-987-7000
Parker: 303-841-0353
Wheat Ridge: 303-231-1308

County Parks:
Adams County
Department of Parks and Community Resources:
303-637-8000, www.co.adams.co.us
Arapahoe County:
Arapahoe County Open Space, Parks and Trails
720-874-6500, www.co.arapahoe,co.us
Boulder County:
Boulder County Parks and Open Space
303-441-3950, www.co.boulder.co.us/open
Douglas County:
Douglas County Open Space and Natural Resources,
Douglas County Parks:
303-660-7495, www.co.douglas.co.us
El Paso County:
El Paso County Parks and Leisure Services
719-520-6389, www.elpasoco.com/parks
Jefferson County:
Jefferson County Opens Space Parks
303-271-5925, www.co.jefferson.co.us

State and National Parks:
Colorado State Parks:
303-866-3437, www.parks.state.co.us
Rocky Mountain National Park:
970-586-1206, www.nps.gov/romo/

Riding Colorado Journal

Keep a record of the trails you have ridden!

Date   **Trail**   **Impressions**

Riding Colorado Journal

Keep a record of the trails you have ridden!

Date   **Trail**   **Impressions**